REACHING TO GOD

GREAT TRUTHS FROM THE BIBLE

Volume 1

REACHING TO GOD

GREAT TRUTHS FROM THE BIBLE

Volume 1

By

R. A. MATTHEWS

Editors

Teresa Zintgraff Youhanaie
Alicia Byrd
Jane Charnock
Alice Powell
Janet Davis

"...In the abundance of counselors there is victory."

Proverbs 11:14

The cover photo is of the Glasgow Cathedral in Scotland

Specifically, the cover photo is the chancel and East wall of the choir (also spelled quire). The publisher wishes to thank Glen Collie and the Cathedral for the kind use of the photograph.

NAVI PUBLISHING

The author obtained permission for the use of names and events in this book. Otherwise, all the characters, dialogue, and events herein are completely fictional, and any resemblance to actual persons, living or dead, or to actual dialogue or events is entirely coincidental and unintended. Fictional characters, dialogue, and events have been introduced in the spirit of Jesus' parables and should not be construed as real unless otherwise stated.

Navi Publishing supports churches and Christian groups. This book may be obtained at a wholesale price for your members or for your fundraising activities. **Go to:**

ReachingToGod.com

Second Print Edition June 2017
ISBN:978-1-936851-14-0

PRINTED IN THE US

Acknowledgements

It is a pleasure to have many to thank for this book. I am grateful for the presence of each of you in my life.

To my newspaper publisher, **Moe Pujol**, and to my newspaper editors, **Josh Richards** and **Jay Thomas**: This book would not have flourished had you each not believed in me and kept publishing my thoughts. Thank you!

To **Preston Boutwell**, who made Bobby run and get a newspaper, and then shoved it at me, insisting I write something: Thank you. The Lord was in that moment!

I want to extend great love and appreciation to my editors: **Teresa Zintgraff Youhanaie, Alicia Byrd, Jane Charnock, Alice Powell,** and **Janet Davis.** You have my heartfelt thanks! You each gave generously of your time to proofread each word and then to send me notes. The book was truly a collaborative effort.

I must add, none of these bright, well-educated women should be blamed when I deviate from proper English grammar. Trust me, Ms. Alice made sure I knew better.

My thanks to **David Ellis**, who kept me from leaving my great little town, bringing me back to the house I adore.

A huge thank you to **Glen Collie** and the **Glasgow Cathedral** in Scotland for granting written permission for the use of the exquisite cover photo. It's amazing!

I want to extend love and appreciation to my **Church Family** at **First Methodist.** Thank you for including me each week. I have come to love each of you individually. Your steadfast encouragement has meant more than I can say. Thank you!

A huge note of appreciation to the Patriarchs—**Mickey, Hoss, Bobby, Buddy, Danny, Pete, Lamar, Kenny, Preston,** and **John**—men of great faith, who lead by example. Thank you for including me. Iron sharpens iron.

Finally, to my pre-readers, **Rev. Pierce Mcintyre, Emily Mead,** and **Rebecca Brannon**: Your comments were always very helpful. Thank you for giving your time to this work!

Dedicated to my mom and dad,
who gave me everything.

Dedicated also to Jay Thomas, Preston Boutwell, and David Ellis.

TABLE OF CONTENTS

INTRODUCTION

Years ago, I heard a comedian making fun of his grandmother because she had a picture of Jesus hanging on her wall.

What's wrong with that? I thought, listening as the audience laughed.

Oh, apparently not everyone loves pictures of the Lord.

I have many. My favorite is "Jesus laughing." I have two—one for home, one for office. Also in my collection is a really old picture of Jesus kneeling in the Garden of Gethsemane. I could never part with it.

I also have quotes from the Bible displayed in the kitchen, bathroom, bedroom, study—wherever I spend time. My favorite: "'I know the plans I have for you,' declares the Lord, 'plans to prosper you and not to harm you, plans to give you hope and a future." Jer. 29:11 (NIV)

Honestly, I always want to be reminded of my faith. It is my greatest comfort.

I have never felt different from my friends. I grew up in a close-knit neighborhood. We all walked to school—that sort of environment. It never occurred to me to ask where my young friends went to church, or if they went to church. I think most did.

Looking back now, I imagine my home life was different from that of my friends. But you don't realize this—you assume everyone lives the same way.

My mom's mom was an ordained minister, but both of my grandmothers were very devout. Their love for the Lord greatly influenced my parents, who passed their devotion along to my brother and me.

When I left for school each day, my mom made sure *A Mighty Fortress Is Our God* was playing, wafting around my brother and me, following us out the door. At the time, I hardly noticed, but now I see how deliberate it was.

At big family dinners, my cousins and I washed dishes as we sang hymns. I remember planning a family funeral with a new pastor, who didn't know my family. I suggested *In the Garden* for the grave-side service.

"Oh, no," he said. "We won't have hymnals."

I smiled. "Don't worry, we know all the verses."

When my aunt wanted to thank me for helping her, she bought me a new Bible. You don't want to know how many Bibles I own.

I was chosen over all my cousins and second cousins to inherit the cherished family heirloom. That precious piece is my grandmother's prayer table. Only one grandchild could get it, and my aunt (the Bible-giver above) passed it to me, deciding I was "the one."

I am the envy of my cousins over this, trust me.

Both of my sincere grandmothers appear in stories in this book. In fact, many in my family will make their presence known. These 24 columns, first published in my local newspaper, were written between 2015 and 2017. They reflect not just my walk with my heavenly Father, but the faith of those in my family who walked with Him long before I was born. It is the Presence of God through these many generations that radiates across the pages of this book.

I know growing up in such an environment gave me a head start, and I am grateful. I am also thankful to have had the opportunity to write these great truths. Landing in my town and writing the first article came from out of the blue. It was a turning point, as you will see.

I hope the truths in this book will bless you as much as they have blessed me.

Part I

Great Truths

"Unto thee, O God, do we give thanks…"

PSALM 75:1

- 1 -

MARY AND ELIZABETH

TWO WOMEN WHO CELEBRATE BEFORE CHRISTMAS

"…nothing is impossible with God."

LUKE 1:37[1]

[1] NLT

Two Women Who Celebrate Before Christmas

As a rule of thumb, you don't want to make an angel mad. But he did just that. And, honestly, it was so unlike him. The Bible describes this faithful old priest as "righteous before God, walking blamelessly in all the commandments and statutes of the Lord."

So what went wrong?

It seems the old man had his heart set on having a child before he died. He prayed earnestly to God year after year. Then, suddenly, an angel appears to him in the temple and says, "Do not be afraid, Zechariah, for your prayer has been heard."

The angel says his old, barren wife will give birth to a son and to name him John. "And he will...make ready for the Lord a people prepared."

That's where the trouble began—the holy man didn't believe the angel.

It gets worse. This was not your run-of-the-mill heavenly host.

"I am Gabriel," the angel announces. I can see him arching to his full height, spreading his massive wings as far as they will go. "I stand in the presence of God."

Oooooh. See what I mean?

Can't you hear the words echoing off the gold and marble of the temple? This old priest needed to know with whom he was dealing.

And here it comes.

"Behold, you will be silent," Gabriel announces. "Unable to speak until the day these things take place, because you did not believe my words..."

Gabriel leaves, and six months later he is given the highest honor in heaven: Gabriel is sent with a message for a virgin. And what were her final words to him?

Mary says, "May it be done to me according to your word."

Many think when Mary learns she will give birth by the Holy Spirit that she keeps quiet, only telling Joseph to whom she's engaged.

Not so.

Immediately, she hurries into the hill country to an old woman. When Mary steps inside her home, the woman shouts, "Blessed are you among women, and blessed is the fruit of your womb!"

This is Mary's beloved cousin, Elizabeth. Obviously Elizabeth knows Mary is carrying the Messiah. The old woman's words burst forth, coming from the Holy Spirit. "And why is this granted to me, that the mother of my Lord should come to me?"

These two women are similarly situated: one too old to give birth yet six months pregnant, the other a virgin, yet also with child. The impossible made possible.

Mary will stay with her cousins, Elizabeth and, yes, old Zechariah, until their child arrives. Six months later Jesus will be born.

Many believe this was a fearful time for Mary.

Not so.

The Biblical accounts of those months don't say this. On the contrary, Luke paints a vivid picture of Mary celebrating. He writes of her singing, "My soul exalts the Lord...the Mighty One has done great things for me..."

And why not celebrate?

Both women know the prophecies, hundreds of years old:

"A voice cries, 'In the wilderness, prepare the way of the LORD; make straight in the desert a highway for our God.'" Isaiah 40:3

"Behold, a virgin will be with child and bear a son, and she will call his name Immanuel." Isaiah 7:14

Both Mary and Elizabeth now know who, when, and where—it's an exciting time! Can't you see the two cooking and singing, dancing and praising God, chatting joyously?

And then there is poor old Zechariah, who can't utter a peep—because he did not trust God.

Don't make that same mistake. Believe! When you earnestly pray, believe!

Listen to the final words Gabriel speaks to Mary. Memorize them.

"...nothing is impossible with God."[2]

---

[2] The quotations were taken from the following translations: Luke 1:19 (ESV), Luke 1:20 (ESV), Luke 1:38 (NAS), Luke 1:19 (ESV), Luke 1:42 (NIV), Luke 1:38 (ESV), Luke 1:47,49 (NASB), Isaiah 40:3 (ESV), Isaiah 7:14 (NASB), Luke 1:37 (NLT), respectively.

- 2 -

JEREMIAH

YOU NEVER FAIL UNTIL YOU GIVE UP

"'For I know the plans I have for you,' declares the Lord, 'plans to prosper you and not to harm you, plans to give you hope and a future.'"

JEREMIAH 29:11[3]

[3] NIV

You Never Fail Until You Give Up

A hijacking occurred in the South recently. This sort of thing happens, and it happened in a small, country town at the local First United Methodist Church.

"Hijacking 101" isn't taught in seminary. You are never going to be prepared, but the minister rose to the occasion, obviously bringing his life experience to bear on the situation. He stepped toward the outlaw and invited the boy to pray.

The desperado clearly had been raised in a Christian home.

I couldn't see as well as others at the scene, but I suspect the whole congregation wondered what would happen next.

The tow-haired boy immediately responded to the request for prayer—all of his three-year-old self. He had carried off the children's sermon, effervescing with one comment after another, the pastor unable to get a word in edgewise. But the tyke surrendered when asked to pray.

"Thank you," the boy began, "for food...and...the church...and...my toys..."

There were lots of "ands"—he was a thankful child. When the boy finally finished, he turned and raced down the aisle to his proud parents, beaming.

The whole church grinned.

Joy erupted again when the pastor began the sermon, explaining how seminary hadn't prepared him for hospital visitations either. It seems patients tend to undress to show off their scars.

But the sermon was about scars of a different kind—the emotional ones we carry through life. Our failures.

I leaned forward. Who can't relate to this? I'm a Baptist and we shout "Amen!" when the Spirit moves us. You learn early on that whole congregations of Methodists and Presbyterians will turn and stare at such behavior. Gratefully I remembered this, gently stifling my enthusiasm, but inside I was busting out with one "Amen!" after another. Perhaps I need a flag to wave vigorously at such times.

As he preached, famous failures came to mind.

Dick Cheney flunked out of Yale—twice. Jerry Seinfeld was jeered off stage at his first comedy club.

You'll remember the famous line said about Fred Astaire: "Can't act. Can't sing. Slightly bald. Can dance a little."

Harrison Ford was told he couldn't make it, and Marilyn Monroe was advised by modeling agents to become a secretary.

Steven Spielberg failed to get into film school at USC three times. In fact, he never got in.

Stephen King's *Carrie* was rejected 30 times, and Monet was mocked for impressionism.

Elvis was fired from the Grand Ole Opry and told, "You ain't goin' nowhere, son."

Harry Truman's business went bankrupt. Henry Ford failed five times, until he finally succeeded with his Ford Motor Company.

Think Macy's department store, think seven unsuccessful businesses beforehand.

Bill Gates dropped out of Harvard and his first company, Traf-O-Data, failed. Obviously he didn't quit.

Colonel Sander's famous chicken recipe was rejected over 1,000 times before succeeding.

Walt Disney was told he "lacked imagination." He also didn't let bankruptcy after bankruptcy stop him.

Einstein was deemed mentally handicapped.

The Wright brothers failed repeatedly with their flying machines. Nobel-prize winning Churchill flunked the sixth grade and was defeated at every try for public office before he was elected Prime Minister. And perhaps the most famous failure was Thomas Edison who made 1,000 tries at the light bulb. What if he'd quit at the 600th failure? Could we have blamed him?

Michael Jordan missed more than 9,000 baskets—twenty-six of those would have been game-winning shots. He said, "I have failed over and over again in my life. And that is why I succeed."

The minister skillfully aborted the hijacking of his service that day by asking the child to pray. Prayer is also the answer to failure.

There's one particular area of my life where I'm a complete failure. I try, I fail. I try again, I fail again. And I try yet again. You can come to a point where you think it's hopeless.

After church, I talked the matter over with God and am starting anew. Prayer will change your heart.

The prophet Jeremiah had been thrilled when he found the law book in the temple, the main part of Deuteronomy, thinking it would change the people's lives. Subsequently, he realized people can't change their ways until they change their heart. And for a change of heart you need God.

I find great comfort and hope in the words God gave Jeremiah:

"For I know the plans I have for you," declares the Lord, "plans to prosper you and not to harm you, plans to give you hope and a future."[4]

The Methodist pastor concluded his sermon that Sunday morning by assuring his congregation that God says, "Do it again! Do it again! Do it again!"

Remember, you never fail until you give up.

---

[4] Jer. 29:11 (NIV)

- 3 -

BOAZ

HE JUST WANTED TO HELP HER

"Give and it will be given to you."

LUKE 6:38[5]

[5] NIV

He Just Wanted to Help Her

Initially, he just wanted to help her.

It was spring in Bethlehem and the fields of gold were ripe for harvest. His men were already cutting the barley when he spotted her, working alongside his women, gathering the leftover crop.

"Whose young woman is this?" he asks his foreman and learns Ruth is a widow from a neighboring country, now living in Bethlehem for a noble reason.

"She has [worked] from early morning until now," the foreman says, "except for a short rest."

Immediately, Boaz leaves his foreman and goes to Ruth—she needed to know there was danger in other fields, men who would assault her.

"Keep close to my young women," he says. "When you are thirsty . . . drink [water] the young men have drawn."

"Why?" She doesn't understand his kindness.

Boaz says he learned how her in-laws left Bethlehem during a famine. Their sons married and died. So did the father. The old mother, alone now, wanted to return home, and Ruth had left everything to come with her mother-in-law.

Boaz is impressed.

At mealtime, he invites her to eat with them and quietly tells his men to leave extra crop behind for her.

When Ruth goes home that night, laden with grain, she tells Naomi, her mother-in-law, the day's events.

"The man is a close relative of ours," Naomi replies, "one of our redeemers."

A redeemer was a relative who married a childless widow, like Ruth, so an heir could be born to inherit the land.

Ruth continues working throughout the harvest, and then her mother-in-law devises a plan to assure her daughter-in-law's security. Ruth does as she's told—getting dressed, going to where Boaz and his men are threshing grain, and hiding until nightfall. Once Boaz falls asleep, she uncovers his feet and lies down. He's startled in the night and realizes a woman is at his feet.

"Who are you?" he asks. It was pitch dark.

"I am Ruth . . . spread your wings . . . for you are a redeemer."

Whoa! She's asking him to marry her!

Honestly, when you read this book, you wonder if Naomi was a tad bit crazy. Why didn't they invite him for dinner? Can you imagine any woman lying beside her employer at midnight? Then asking him to marry her!

Even Naomi didn't know how this would end. She had told her daughter-in-law, "He will tell you what to do."

Ruth knew Boaz had felt pity for her, but that didn't mean he'd welcome a proposal on a threshing floor in the middle of the night. He could say, "Go home!"

I bet you want me to get on with it. What does Boaz do?

He accepts!

"May you be blessed by the Lord," he says. Then Boaz adds something more interesting. "You have made this last kindness greater than the first..."

The first was leaving her family to return with her mother-in-law, but how is this proposal a kindness? A poor, young widow wanting a wealthy landowner?

Here it is, listen to what Boaz says. "You have not gone after young men..."

Boaz felt bad about his age.

We all have such insecurities—things we can't change, things we feel another may reject. Some are obvious like age or size, but others are hidden—a disease, a debt, a conviction, impotence.

Boaz is thrilled. He doesn't care about his work any longer, quickly leaving the threshing floor to fulfill the complicated requirements to marry Ruth.

"Ruth" is the eighth book of the Bible. Just a fanciful tale, or did these people actually live?

The writer plainly tells us: Ruth's child is Obed, whose son is Jesse, whose son is David (as in slingshot David who fights Goliath). And David becomes King of Israel.

Ruth and Boaz were real people living over 3,000 years ago. You will see them again in Jesus' ancestry, which begins the New Testament.

Boaz helped Ruth and Naomi, expecting nothing in return, but they ended up helping him more. Though a successful man, Boaz was unsure of himself with marriage.

No matter who you are, God will send people in need. The person you help today may help you tomorrow. This is God's way.

Jesus said, "Give and it will be given to you." [6]

---

[6] The quotations in this section were taken from the ESV translation of the Holy Bible: Ruth 2:5, 2:7, 2:8, 2:9, 2:20, 3:9, 3:9, 3:4, 3:10, 3:10, and Luke 6:38, respectively.

- 4 -

Joseph

Ready for God to Show You the Future?

"Trust in the Lord with all your heart and lean not on your own understanding, in all your ways acknowledge Him and He will make straight your paths."

PROVERBS 3: 5-6 [7]

[7] NIV

Ready for God to Show You the Future?

Have you ever felt strangely drawn to act in some way, and only afterward understood why—realizing God had shown you the future?

My grandfather owned a neighborhood grocery store several blocks from the family home. On a dark night my grandmother suddenly grabbed one of his hats, sensing he was in danger. She shoved her hair beneath it, dressed as a man, and hurried to his store. Charging through the front door, she found a robber with my grandfather.

Immediately, the thief bolted and ran.

This grandmother, my mom's mom, was an ordained Nazarene minister, renowned for her faithfulness to God. The Lord showed her the future that night.

In the Bible, the most important person shown the future was Jesus' father.

Preachers and academics alike will tell you we know little about this Joseph. Not so—what the Bible tells us is profound. Joseph is the person in Scripture whom God trusted above all others. God's revelations to Joseph clearly show this.

Jesus may have lain in a manger before doting wise men and surrounded by the gentle bleating of lambs, but imminent evil threatened our Lord.

Newborns, babies crawling on hands and knees, and toddlers taking their first steps—all would soon be ripped from their mothers' arms and murdered. Jesus should have been among them, but an angel came to Joseph in a dream saying, "...flee into Egypt, and stay there until I tell you, for Herod will seek the young child to destroy him."[8]

It must have felt bizarre to Joseph—the virgin birth, the bright star hovering above, the wise men bringing treasure. Why leave such a celebration?

"Just a dream!" his family may have said. "Egypt is a long way. You don't know anyone there. Why go?"

Joseph knew exactly why—God had shown him the future.

See the level of trust between the two. That didn't happen overnight. Joseph had shown his loyalty to God for a lifetime, and God trusted him above all others. That's big!

The Bible doesn't have to tell us the strength of the relationship between God and Joseph. It's obvious. God had to be sure the father of our Lord would not hesitate, would not doubt each angel in each dream—the life of baby Jesus depended on it.

There were four dreams in all. First, that Mary would give birth via the Holy Spirit, which sounds common to us, but Joseph needed real conviction to believe this one. He needed real conviction for the second one as well—to quickly flee. The final two

[8] Mt. 2:13 (World English Bible)

dreams were to return, and then to settle in a safe area.[9]

Many in the Bible knew of impending events. Elijah knew of the coming drought, Daniel knew of the destruction of the temple, and Samuel knew Saul would lose his kingdom. Like Joseph, they were men chosen to do great things.

But God also calls in the smallest of things.

Take the man with the jug, living 2,000 years ago.

He felt strangely drawn to the edge of the city where he met two men. They followed him home and spoke with the head of the household, asking to see the guest room.

Only later would the man with the jug know the role he played for God. Jesus arrived that evening with the twelve and ate dinner in that upstairs room. It was the Last Supper.

The two men who had followed the man with the jug were Peter and John. Jesus had told these two disciples that a man with a jar of water would be waiting for them at the edge of the city and would lead them to the house. Jesus had also told Peter and John to approach the master of the house, to ask to be shown the large, furnished upper room.[10]

Jesus knew all of this would happen. The man with the jug had no idea. He only knew that he felt led to meet two men at the edge of the city.

Must you be special to be led by God? The man with the jug isn't even named in the Bible.

---

[9] Mt. 1:20; 2:13, 19-20, 22

[10] Luke 22:7-13

Perhaps, as the years passed, he forgot about his deed. I hope not—he was specially chosen to act for the Lord. God must have known when He placed the deed in this man's heart, that the man would obey.

You too may be guided by a feeling, a vision, a dream, or a series of events too coincidental to be sheer coincidence. You may even be led by a miracle.

Draw close to God every day. Pray to understand His way of speaking to you. As you learn to see Him leading, and then act upon His guidance, trust will develop. It's the kind of trust my grandmother, Joseph, and the man with the jug shared with God. The kind that led all three to act without question.

The more you trust and act upon God's leading, the more you will be shown.

"Trust in the Lord with all your heart and lean not on your own understanding. In all your ways acknowledge him and he will make straight your paths."[11]

---

[11] Prov. 3:5-6 (NIV)

-5-

ISAIAH

THE BAREFOOT AND BARE BUTTOCKS BILLBOARD

"You shall have no other gods before me."

EXODUS 20:3[12]

[12] NASB

The Barefoot and Bare Buttocks Billboard

It's not *Daniel and the Lion's Den* nor *David and Goliath.* It's a lesser known Bible story—*Barefoot and Bare Buttocks.*

I gasped the first time I read it.

A holy man walked naked and barefoot among the Israelites for three whole years.

Immediately I took a survey, wondering who else knew.

No one.

"Was he crazy?" I was asked over and over again.

No. Nor is he an obscure fellow. I think both Jesus and the Apostle Paul quote him more than any other prophet. When John the Baptist proclaims, "I am a voice of one crying in the wilderness, 'Make straight the way of the Lord,'"[13] those words were written by this prophet 700 years earlier.

It's Isaiah.

Did I hear you gasp?

Exactly!

---

[13] John 1: 23 (NASB)

I think of him as a grand person. Isaiah wrote: "For unto us a child is born, unto us a Son is given...and his name shall be called Wonderful..."[14]

Handel placed that amazing prophecy in his musical masterpiece, *The Messiah*.

Yet, in the 20th chapter of Isaiah, the prophet drops his drawers (technically, it's sackcloth). Isaiah goes barefoot and naked for three years. Can you imagine your children staring at the sight of a wandering naked preacher? For three years!

And why?

God has a point to make and Isaiah is chosen. The prophet becomes God's human ad—a T.V. commercial without the television, a billboard display without the billboard.

But naked?

This message was that important. God wanted to make sure no one forgot it. Here's what happened.

Assyrian King Tiglath-Pileser III has conquered most of the known world. My kitten is named Tiglath-Pileser IV due to a similar marauding nature.

Northern Israel then rebels against Assyria, turning to Egypt for help. The Lord and His commandments are cast aside. There's such wickedness the people even burn their children as offerings to gods.

The Lord is furious—so angry He destroys the northern kingdom of Israel, allowing Assyria to take those Israelites into captivity. No one is left except the tribe of Judah in the south.

This is why God called Isaiah to walk naked. It's a warning for Judah not to trust Egypt.

---

[14] Isaiah 9:6 KJV

The Lord says: "As my servant Isaiah has walked naked and barefoot for three years as a sign…against Egypt…so shall the king of Assyria lead away the Egyptian captives…naked and barefoot, with buttocks uncovered…"[15]

Hezekiah, king of Judah, gets the message: If God's people don't return to Him, they too will be taken captive, led away barefoot with bare buttocks. Hezekiah institutes massive reform to win God's favor, and the people do all that Hezekiah asks.

Years pass.

One day hundreds of thousands of mighty Assyrian soldiers arrive at the gates of Jerusalem, the capital of Judah. I know—it's unbelievable!

An Assyrian officer then stands outside the city saying, "Behold, you are trusting in Egypt, that broken reed…"[16]

He shouts to surrender or face the consequences.

God's people are afraid. Terrified. What are they going to do? Assyria has conquered everything in sight and is promising some leniency if they will come out.

But they recall that human billboard. Who could forget it? You know they gasped like I did, except they actually saw the naked prophet—on a regular basis. Certainly they stopped and stared more than once as Isaiah walked by in the buff.

God wanted them to stare, wanted His warning emblazoned on their memories. They had to SEE their future—they were doomed if they didn't have faith.

Judah's King Hezekiah petitions Isaiah, and the prophet looks into the future. Listen to what Isaiah

---

[15] Isaiah 20:3-4 (ESV)

[16] Isaiah 36:6 (ESV)

says: "[The Assyrian king] shall hear a rumor and return to his own land, and I will make him fall by the sword in his own land."[17]

Indeed, the mighty Assyrian king believes there's a homeland insurrection and immediately abandons his siege of Jerusalem. He returns home, and he is later assassinated.

God's people had changed their ways, and God granted them His favor.

I'm not facing Assyrian pillage (unless you count Tiglath-Pileser IV), but I want God's favor more than anything. I know to stay right with Him. We all know.

Hopefully we won't look out tomorrow and see a wandering, naked prophet. But this nation needs to turn back to holiness. Really needs it.

Turning away from God is defeat, staying close to God leads to success.

---

[17] 2Kings 19:7 (ESV)

- 6 -

JUDAH

PERHAPS YOUR LIFE IS BETTER THAN YOU THINK IT IS

"I always thank my God…"

1 COR. 1:4[18]

[18] World English Bible

Perhaps Your Life Is Better Than You Think It Is

Just this one thing, and then I'll be happy. Ever thought that?

Cindy's puppy, lean and long-legged, cleared fences like a deer. Luckily, Alpha was a good-natured dog. No one really cared that he cheerfully roamed the neighborhood. At least, not then.

Alpha's only vice was chewing the newspaper.

"If I could just break him," Cindy said, "I'd be happy."

Every morning she'd wave the torn newspaper, scolding him badly until Alpha finally stopped.

"Good boy!" Cindy praised him with treats.

Next morning, the newspaper was nicely intact, but Alpha stood over three more papers, wagging his tail.

"No, no!" she said, shaking the extra newspapers.

The dog covered his head with his paws. Clearly, he'd disappointed her.

Next morning, Cindy sighed with relief. Only Alpha and one newspaper lay on the front porch.

Wheww!

She glanced toward the sidewalk—evenly spaced, in a neat row, lay 15 newspapers.

Cindy said, "I didn't realize how good my life was."

Alpha now lives in the country with a nice old couple.

Ten brothers also thought one thing would bring them happiness. Their half-brother, Joe, was 17 at the time, and they hated him.

I'm not sure whether it was Joe's fault. They all worked together in their father's business, and the old man had given Joe the job of bringing him reports.

Perhaps the boy was too diligent—what the brothers might have labeled "disloyal"—since Joe took home bad reports about them. Maybe the teen also lacked judgment. He'd relay his dreams, suggesting that everyone in the family would admire him one day.

Whether you call it a "straightforward manner" or "tattling and bragging," neither was the final straw.

That came from their father.

Understand the dynamics of this blended family. Joe's mother was the only woman the boys' father ever loved. And she had died. I think each time the old man looked into Joe's eyes, there was his beloved wife. Simply put, this father treasured Joe more than his other boys, which hurt the ten deeply.

The day of reckoning finally comes.

Joe arrives at work in a brand-new, expensive coat, and the men snap. They'll never be happy until he's dead. Yes, the ten plot to kill Joe.

It's Judah, third oldest and the brother they all listen to, who changes the boy's fate. Judah decides to relocate Joe to a faraway home—not nearly as nice as Alpha's.

You may recognize this as the Bible story *Joseph's Coat of Many Colors.*

The brothers promptly sell Joseph to a caravan of traders, dip that precious coat in blood, and take it to their father.

Problem solved. Brat gone. Everyone lives happily ever after.

No.

The old man wept and wept.

His daughters come to him, but Jacob refuses to be comforted. "I'll die mourning my son."

What the brothers thought would bring happiness didn't at all.

The old man's sorrow hits Judah the hardest. I imagine Judah watching his father cry, seeing the old man's body bent with grief. Judah knows what he's done. He remembers how their lives had been when Joseph had filled the old man with happiness.

This is perhaps the most heart-wrenching story of the Old Testament. Judah will eventually choose to leave his wife and sons for slavery in another country, rather than bring more grief to his father.[19]

Maybe what you think will bring you happiness isn't what you need at all.

A Bible teacher asked, "What if you woke up tomorrow, and all you had was what you'd thanked God for yesterday?"

Wow!

Cherish all that you have. Perhaps your life is better than you think it is.

---

[19] Gen. 37-44

- 7 -

MY MOM

MY MOM'S MAGIC CAN BE YOUR MAGIC

"…David would take his harp and play it…and Saul would be refreshed and be well…"

1 SAMUEL 16:23[20]

[20] NASB

My Mom's Magic Can Be Your Magic

"This year," he said. "This coming year you will be dead."

He wasn't a fortune teller—he was a doctor. An oncologist.

He sat by her hospital bed on Christmas Eve, having never seen her before. She had been in a car accident and routine tests showed Stage-IV breast cancer.

She looked at him and smiled.

"Do you understand?" he asked in earnest. I think perhaps he moved closer, but I can't remember exactly.

I sat in a chair at the foot of her bed.

"You don't know," I said, my voice filled with belligerence. "You don't."

This was my mom. My dad had died the year before, and she was all I had left.

He ignored me, focusing on her, explaining her upcoming demise. I think he said he had a "moral obligation" to tell her. I only think that because we heard it so often.

She kept smiling at him, which bewildered the good doctor. But this part was clear to me—my mom was not interested in his predictions. No one told her what to think.

A second specialist appeared the next morning—Christmas day. They were opening radiation oncology just for her. He told me to call hospice, to get her on the waiting list.

"She'll be dead by February," he said. He had a responsibility to tell us.

We saw more doctors for one reason or another.

"You are going to die very soon," each said, making clear their obligation.

She didn't die in February. Not in March, April, May, or June. Month after month passed.

I watched as my mom's oncologist gave her the very best care, and I grew to both love and trust him. Accordingly, I took his Christmas Eve prediction more seriously, yet it was confusing to me.

"Will it be like a time bomb?" I asked as the next Christmas approached. She seemed much better to me, but I didn't know anything about cancer. "You said a year," I continued. "Will she die without warning?"

He shook his head, saying she was no longer on a death time-line. She was getting better.

No other doctor agreed with him. We saw a heart specialist when the oncologist detected a murmur.

"She should be dead," the cardiologist announced.

So did the next three and all of the general practitioners. As I said, so many moral obligations.

My guess is that most patients would have been at least discouraged, if not depressed. And my mom did almost die—more than once. Yet her attitude never wavered. I never saw her feel sorry for herself. Nothing got the best of my mom. Not ever.

She had a great relationship with God, and they had an unspoken secret. She employed God's holy magic in times of distress.

Magic?

From God?

What was that?

Honestly, I should have known long before I did. At the brisk age of two, I was introduced to choir. There were probably seven or eight of us—the two year olds. We had little lemon-colored robes with big red bows at the neck.

"You were the choir," my mom said.

According to her, as long as I sang, everyone sang. And when I stopped, everyone stopped.

"You would see a lady's hat," my mom said, "and get distracted."

Apparently, the choir director quickly waved to me, and I was back, bringing along the two year olds.

For a decade choir was my joy, but at twelve I wanted out. That's when I had a rude awakening—choir was not optional, it was mandatory. No amount of pleading worked with my mom, not about choir.

Like I said, I should have caught on.

As I write this, Christmas morning, I am listening to Handel's *Messiah* and thinking of the last time I was at that concert with her.

When I left for school, *A Mighty Fortress Is Our God* was always playing.

Do you see the theme? Long before scientists proved that music could help stroke patients recover, or that music greatly improved motor skills in those with neurological damage—my mom instinctively knew it was potent.

She loved the Gaither specials with their Southern Gospel music, and that became a daily treat during her illness.

The week of Christmas, four years from that fateful Christmas Eve, my mom passed to the Lord.

She never said it, but holy music was her magic. She believed it would get you through when nothing else could. That it could brighten, embolden, and inflate the deflated ball of life. And it does.

Don't take my word, try it.

For a paltry $2.19 as I write this in 2015, you can have *Handel's Messiah by the London Philharmonic Choir and Orchestra* as an easy digital download from Amazon.

The whole thing!

You can put it right on your phone!

50 Classic Hymns by various artists and *Come to the Quiet* by John Michael Talbot are also my staples.

I like Southern Gospel, but I find joy in a boatload of contemporary Christian music: just about anything by Steven Curtis Chapman; *8 Greatest Hits* by Phillips, Craig, and Dean; *Welcome to the New* by Mercy Me; "Come Away" and "Rooftops" - Jesus Culture; "Just Say Jesus" - 7eventh Time Down; "Come to the Well," "Thrive," and "Until the Whole World Knows" - Casting Crowns; "Steady my Heart" - Kari Jobe; "Love Come to Life" - Big Daddy Weave; "I Need a Miracle" - Third Day; "All the People Said Amen" - Matt Maher; "Live Like That" - Sidewalk Prophet; "By Your Side" - Tenth Avenue North.

Remember, I wrote this list in 2015. Many new and wonderful artists have arrived since then. Lauren Daigle is my favorite new discovery: I love "Once and for All" and "I Am Yours."

This year, let holy music lift you, heal you, brighten your life. It's nothing short of magic.

- 8 -

JEHU

THE SEXIEST MAN ALIVE!

"A good name is more desirable than great riches."

PROVERBS 22:1[21]

[21] NIV

The Sexiest Man Alive!

Had there been a "Hebrew People Magazine" or "Holy Land Enquirer," his picture would have rocked the cover as the "Sexiest Man Alive!" The Bible says you knew he was coming long before you saw him—he drove his chariot that furiously.

The man is Jehu, an Israeli army commander.

He could aim his bow and pierce the heart of an enemy without stopping.

A man's man—definitely.

But I suspect old women with wide, toothless grins stared as he passed.

Can't you see him strutting toward battle, tall and broad shouldered, wearing his armor like a second skin? I certainly would have sought an introduction, smiling a little longer than necessary.

Jehu's life is about to intersect with that of a young prophet. The two will change history.

It's roughly 800 years before the birth of Christ. Israel is at war with Syria and encamped at Ramoth-gilead along the border. The Israeli commanders are in conference when the young prophet appears.

"I have a word for you, O commander," the prophet announces.

Prophets were revered. When one said, "Thus says the Lord," everyone stopped and listened. These were the very words of God—the red letters of the Old Testament.

Even so, I think those commanders looked over this guy and not in a good way. He had tied up his robes so his naked legs were free beneath them. I'm not making this up, he did that.

Jehu then asks which commander the prophet wants.

"You, O commander."

So Jehu and the ill-dressed prophet step inside the house.

Minutes later, the prophet throws open the door and flees.

What do you bet Jehu's burly men guffawed—watching the man racing into the night in his mini skirt? Listen to what they say:

"Is all well? Why did this mad fellow come to you?"

Ah, the plot thickens—Jehu doesn't tell them!

"You know the fellow and his talk," Jehu says.

But these soldiers, willing to fight to the death for Jehu, know something is up.

"That is not true," they say. "Tell us now."

Here's what I haven't said. This prophet is scared to death. He'd been sent by the great Elisha who'd told him to tie up his robes and flee after completing the dangerous mission.

So what happened in that closed room?

Treason.

"'Thus says the Lord,'" Jehu tells his men, repeating the prophet's words. "'I anoint you king over Israel.'"

Suddenly there's uproar! Every man stands and throws his garments on the steps before Jehu.

"Jehu is king!" they proclaim, blowing the trumpet.

Jehu steadies them. "If this is your decision, then let no one slip out of the city..."

No one can warn the evil king.

Jehu mounts his chariot, and a company of men follows him.

Hours later, at the king's city, the watchman on the wall announces that men are coming. He can't tell who they are, so the king sends out a horseman.

Jehu shouts for the horseman to get in line behind him.

The watchman relays what's happening, yet he still can't see who is leading the company. But listen to what he says:

"The driving is like the driving of Jehu...for he drives furiously."

I told you!

The king quickly races his chariot past the strong walls to meet his general, undoubtedly thinking there's news from battle. Upon reaching Jehu, the king suddenly realizes treason is afoot, turns his royal chariot, and runs.

You know how this ends.

Jehu draws his bow with all his strength. The arrow slices between the evil king's shoulders and pierces his heart.

Jehu, known as a man of strength and courage, lived up to his reputation that day. The Bible says even a child is known by his deeds.

One of the best parts of living in a small, Southern town is that people are "known." You live and die by your reputation. Especially if you own a business.

What do you want to be known for?

Me? I want to be that nameless, little guy with the naked, white legs in the mini skirt. I want to be known as one who speaks for God.

And you? Stop and consider this—what's most important to you? Live your life that way. Consciously make a choice every day for the reputation you want.

"A good name is more desirable than great riches."[22]

---

[22] The Scripture quotations in this section were taken from the following translations of the Holy Bible: 2Kings 9:5 (ESV), 2Kings 9:5 (ESV); 2Kings 9:11 (ESV), 2Kings 9:11 (ESV), 2Kings 9:12 (ESV), 2Kings 9:6 (ESV), 2Kings 9:13 (ESV), 2Kings 9:15 (ESV), 2Kings 9:20 (NASB), and Proverbs 22:1 (NIV), respectively.

- 9 -

Balaam

When Balaam's Bad Ass Got Three Whoopings

"Choose this day whom you will serve…But as for me and my house, we will serve the Lord."

JOSHUA 24:15[23]

[23] ESV

When Balaam's Bad Ass Got Three Whoopings!

This is the story of three ass whoopings. Balaam should have learned his lesson, but did he?

I shouted aloud in the exam room of my eye-doctor's office last Thursday—no butt whoopings in progress. Thankfully. I was alone, door closed, Bible in hand. I'd just read that Balaam, son of Beor, was killed by the Israelites.[24]

"No!" I said. "Can't be. Not my Balaam!"

This Balaam, son of Beor, had to be different from my Balaam.

Dr. Carter entered in the midst of my crisis.

"Have to find something," I said, nose in my Bible. "Not the same one..." I babbled on.

If you've never heard of Balaam, the famous first-century historian Josephus called him the greatest prophet of his time. I love those who speak for God, so I loved Balaam. Obviously.

But wait, was I missing something?

Here's the story of Balaam—the Balaam I knew. It's found in Numbers, the 4th book of the Bible.

God's people had left slavery in Egypt, wandered 40 years, and are now encamped beside the Promised Land in the country of Moab. They've defeated several

---

[24] Joshua 13:22

kings along the way, which makes Moab's King Balak most uncomfortable. Okay, he's scared witless.

King Balak quickly sends for Balaam, determined to hire the famous prophet to curse the Israelites.

Balaam refuses to return with the king's men—God had directed Balaam not to curse the Israelites. Balaam tells the king's men that no amount of money can change his decision.

The king sends princes with more money.

This time God says, "...go with them, but only do what I tell you."

Hmmm. Things are about to get dicey.

On the journey, Balaam's donkey carries him into a field, then into a wall, then sits down in the road. Balaam beats him each time, and the donkey famously turns and speaks to his master. "Am I in the habit of doing this to you?"

Only then does Balaam see the angel with the sword, ready to kill him.

Immediately, Balaam says, "...if it's evil...I will turn back."

"Go with the men," the angel says, "but speak only the word that I tell you."

What is going on? First Balaam can't go, then God says Balaam can go, and now an angel is about to behead the prophet.

Honestly, I never understood this passage, but I do now. Come along with me.

So the prophet arrives and carefully speaks for God, refusing to curse the Israelites.

King Balak is not about to give up. Oh, no. He does everything but somersaults backward. The king takes Balaam and they sacrifice to God on seven altars. They do it in three different places.

"Let's try over here," the king says, over and over again, desperate for a different result.

Yet it's always the same. Balaam follows God and refuses to curse the Israelites.

So Balaam was a good guy, right?

I'd always thought so.

Still, this passage about the death of Balaam by the Israelites worried me. I read more carefully, following the notes all over the Bible, trying to grasp Balaam's weakness, if he had one.

I found some things I'd overlooked, references to Balaam being an opportunist.[25] The prophet certainly had opportunity staring him in the face. There's a saying among lawyers: The best client is a rich man who's scared. King Balak was that man—willing to pay anything to get free of the Israelites.

So Balaam had to choose his path.

It's the same today: Great leaders face choices. Some succeed while others fail, destroyed by their weaknesses.

Preachers succumb as well.

It's true for everyone.

Your weakness is often what you don't have and want most. It should shout: "Danger! Danger! Warning! Warning!" Weakness is the place evil can easily enter if it's not cautiously guarded.

The day Balaam's ass (his donkey) got three whoopings was a day of reckoning for Balaam. The angel carrying the sword said, "I have come out to oppose you because your way is perverse..."

What does that mean? After all, God had told Balaam he could go as long as Balaam stuck to God's

---

[25] 2Peter 2:15

message. True, but apparently Balaam had other plans. Way over in the New Testament, Peter says Balaam "loved to earn money by doing wrong."[26]

So the angel was sent to set him straight.

Did Balaam change?

Clearly, he didn't curse the Israelites, but Balaam found a way to technically follow God and also satisfy the king.

The book of Numbers doesn't tell what became of Balaam. That's in Joshua, the passage I was reading in my eye-doctor's office. Balaam, yes my Balaam, was killed by the Israelites. Balaam didn't curse God's people, but the prophet showed King Balak how to do it. The king didn't know the Ten Commandments, didn't know that leading God's people to idols and adultery would turn God against the Israelites. Balaam educated him.[27]

God knows your heart as surely as He knew Balaam's. God will confront you just as He did the prophet. Listen to Him—God can help you overcome anything if you acknowledge and surrender your weakness to Him. Examine your life, and hand your weakness to God while you still can.

Being aware of where you are most likely to go wrong is the first step to change. Lay that at the feet of Jesus. Ask for help. Pray for guidance all day long.

Believe that God's grace is sufficient for you. [28]

---

[26] 2Peter 2:15 (NLT)

[27] Num. 31:14-16, Rev. 2:14, Jude 11

[28] Unless otherwise stated, the Scripture quotations are Numbers 22:20 (ESV), Numbers 22:34 (ESV), Numbers 22:32 (ESV), 2Peter 2:15 (NLT), Numbers 22:35 (ESV), respectively.

- 10 -

THE CANAANITE WOMAN

POUNCE WITH ALL PAWS, WITHOUT PAUSE & HOLD ON

"I will not let you go unless you bless me."

GEN. 32:26[29]

[29] ESV

Pounce With All Paws, Without Pause, and Hold On

Sometimes it's best to fight like a kid.

I started Sunday school when I was two. My grandmother was particular, so I'm sure I was decked out in splendid array—embroidered little dress, white gloves, patent leather shoes, my hair in curls.

Apparently, I didn't want to go—my dad said he had to shove me through the door and then close it quickly. The church has two-way mirrors in Sunday-school rooms, like the kind police use for line-ups.

"We weren't about to leave you," my dad said. "You clung to the doorknob, crying."

They waited and watched. Finally, a little boy approached and slammed a plastic ball up the side of my head. And the war was on!

"You pounced on him with all paws," my dad said. "All you could see were the lace-ruffled panties!"

Can we grapple with God like this, wrestle our Lord and win? You may be surprised at what the Bible says.

Scripture gives many examples of those who followed Jesus, begging for help, but apparently one woman was truly obnoxious. She wasn't merely shouting at our Lord, the Bible says she was *crying* at him, wanting healing for her child.

It must have gone on a long while and finally became intolerable. The disciples don't ask Jesus to get rid of her, they *beg* him.

Our Lord has said nothing throughout the ordeal.

When the disciples stop and implore Him to act, she seizes that moment—quickly coming and kneeling at His feet.

I call her the *Heathen Woman*—she was not a child of God but belonged to people who worshipped evil gods. In fact, God had specifically, repeatedly, and adamantly told His people to have nothing to do with them.

Jesus makes that clear when He speaks to her. "I was sent only to the lost sheep of Israel," He says. "Why should I throw the children's bread to dogs?"

He called her a dog!

A lesser person might have walked away humiliated or thrown Jesus an angry retort. But the heathen woman was too desperate for any of that.

She is famous for saying, "Even the dogs eat the crumbs that fall from their master's table."

And Jesus heals her child.[30]

Admittedly, she didn't actually wrestle God to the mat, but Jacob does. Physically. He wrestles with an angel of God and wins. Not kidding![31]

Good King Hezekiah pleads with God when notified of his impending death, and God gives him fifteen more years.[32]

---

[30]Mt. 15:21-28

[31] Genesis 32:22-30

[32] 2 Kings 20:1-6

Even the downright evil can get their way—the most despised King of Israel repented, and God granted him mercy.[33]

So does this mean God changes?

God is the same yesterday, today, and tomorrow. He is all knowing, all powerful, forever in love with us. God does not change.

Nevertheless, God can choose to do anything He wants.

If He chose to bless a heathen woman and evil King Ahab, He can choose to bless you. God decides.

You can imagine my grandmother's face that Sunday morning. She probably offered me a course in behavior modification. It worked—proud to say I haven't decked any two year olds lately. But that childhood fight demonstrates my God-given qualities: passion and determination. I'm grateful for each.

When my dad, a severe diabetic, was hospitalized for amputation of his toe, he contracted a horrible infection in the hospital and suffered terribly. I expected him to die and refused to leave, staying day and night. No one could love a father more than I loved mine.

In the evening, once he fell asleep, I would take the stairs to the chapel one floor above his room. Night after night, I knelt there and begged the Lord for another six months—I couldn't accept losing him.

That was in November, and my dad recovered well enough to go home.

May 31st, six months later, he died at home.

---

[33] 1Kings 21:20-29

The next year, my mom developed a terminal illness which doctors said would take her within months. She lived four years.

Usually, I pray leaving decisions to God, but I doggedly wrestled with Him for both of their lives. I needed them. And prayer moved His tender heart.

In times of desperate need, fiercely reach for God. Go at it like you did as a kid: Pounce with all paws, without pause, and hold on![34]

[34] The Scripture quotations in this section were taken from the World English Bible translation.

-11-

Solomon

The Destruction of the Golden Age of Israel

"Above all else, guard your heart, for it is the wellspring of life."

PROVERBS 4:23[35]

[35] NIV

The Destruction of the Golden Age of Israel

It was called the golden age of Israel, beginning roughly 1,000 years before Christ. This was the reign of Solomon, King David's son, lasting 40 years.

Scripture says, "King Solomon was greater in riches and wisdom than all the other kings of the earth." The weight of the gold he received yearly was 25 tons. Every world ruler sought to speak with him, coming to hear the wisdom of God.

Pretty impressive.

Yet Solomon's story is one of the great tragedies of the Bible—he destroyed his kingdom by making one mistake. Completely avoidable. Perhaps Solomon knew early on what he'd done wrong when he wrote the Proverb, "Above all else, guard your heart for it is the wellspring of life."[36]

My devout aunt used to scratch her head over the verse. "What does it mean? Jesus wanted us to keep our hearts open."

---

[36] Proverbs 4:23 (NIV)

My aunt didn't understand, but you will see why Solomon thought this was the most important thing: "Above all else..."

As soon as Solomon secures his throne, his first act is to make a treaty with Pharaoh, king of Egypt, and to marry Pharaoh's daughter. Solomon loved many more foreign women tallying up 700 wives and 300 concubines. Yet God had warned the Israelites about the women of Moab, Ammon, Edom, Sidon, and other foreign nations. "You must not intermarry with them because they will surely turn away your hearts after their gods."[37]

Solomon thought he was too wise to let that happen. But once he becomes old, his wives turn his heart toward their gods. He builds altars for these idols and sacrifices to them.

It's unthinkable!

King Solomon violated the first commandment—no other gods—something his father could never have done.

God says because of this evil, Israel will be torn apart.[38]

One of the gods Solomon introduces to the Israelites is Chemosh. Chemosh was worshipped by those in Moab. If you read the story of Balaam's ass in chapter 9, (500 years before Solomon) you'll remember how Moab's King Balak did everything possible to get God to curse the Israelites during the Exodus. I kept

---

[37] 1Kings 11:2 (NIV)

[38] 1Kings 11:6-11

asking myself, "Why didn't King Balak leave Chemosh and accept God since he really believed God was all powerful?"

Moabites did convert and choose God. Remember the famous woman who leaves Moab and accepts the one true God? It's Ruth. Her great grandson is King David. And, ironically, it's her great-great grandson, Solomon, who now introduces Chemosh worship to the Israelites.[39]

God is furious!

So you see, when Solomon wrote: "Above all else, guard your heart...," perhaps he knew his mistake. Your heart can overrule your mind and your will.

The person you marry will bring you closer to God or tear you from Him. Scripture says, "Do not be unequally yoked."[40]

I decided long ago that I wouldn't go out with a man unless I asked where he went to church. That was a mistake.

Why?

They always went to church! Every man could name one right off, leaving out the part that it had been ages ago.

The better question: What was the sermon about last Sunday?

I learned.

Never be ashamed to want someone who loves the Lord. The person who laughs at the sermon question isn't the right person for you. The one who

---

[39] 1Kings 11:7

[40] 2Cor. 6:14

responds with a sincere answer will know why you're asking and respect you for it. Your goal isn't to impress anyone but God.

Even if you are happily married, this message is still for you. Your children, your grandchildren need guidance. More today than ever.

Don't think they don't listen. Talk to them.

Simply put, in matters of the heart be very careful—love can bring happiness or ruin.

Or as Solomon said: "Above all else, guard your heart, for it is the wellspring of life." [41]

[41] Prov. 4:23 (NIV)

- 12 -

My Friend

Hope Lost and Found

"Do not merely look out for your own personal interests, but also for the interests of others."

PHIL. 2:4[42]

[42] NASB

Hope Lost and Found

You never know what a person is going through.

They tooled around in a '57 Chevy, both women approaching eighty, calling one another by their last names: "Kotts" and "Tack." Kotts rode shotgun (she'd never learned to drive), while Tack clutched the wheel in a two-fisted, white-knuckled, we're-good-to-go grip. Tack's coke-bottle glasses told the world she was blind, but no one dared challenge the duo.

Not surprisingly, their granddaughters became lawyers. Age wise, the girls were in five-year stair steps: Take-charge Tara Tack, kind-hearted Kerrie Kotts, and memorable Willa Tack. Pretty and funny, blonde Willa always stood out.

After their grandmothers died, Tara moved into Tack's house and Kerrie into Kotts's—three blocks apart. In fact, Tack's house sits on Kotts Avenue, named for Kerrie Kotts's grandfather. I'm not making this up.

On many nights, Kerrie would find herself sprawled across Tack's hardwood floors. Kerrie's pen would fire across the page, as the more experienced Tara Tack explained a legal procedure.

Lawyering is a complex business, so most attorneys choose specialties. Kerrie gravitated toward clients she called *the patients*.

The patients never dressed up to see her—no lipstick or high heels. Most awakened not realizing their lives were about to change, that someone would be taking them to the courthouse.

They weren't criminals. No. In fact, most seemed helpless. Once they arrived at the courthouse, the Constitution required they be represented. Kerrie would step inside their little rooms, introduce herself, and explain the matter, saying she was there for them.

They came for various reasons, many suicidal.

Kerrie had a counseling background and liked this work. She said people who lose hope kill themselves.

One day Kerrie represented a young mother, clearly exhausted by life. The mother had left her toddler with a cousin while she worked. The child had fought it, kicking and screaming. Only later did the mother learn why—the abuse.

"He's better without me," the mother said, weeping bitterly, hating herself.

Kerrie spoke separately with the woman's parents and sisters. They'd brought the child—his sad eyes said he knew. Kerrie took the adults aside, refusing to talk in front of the boy, then Kerrie went back to the mother. All Kerrie could think was how everyone was continuing to hurt that child.

"He needs you," Kerrie said.

The mother shook her head.

"Do you know what happens to children when a parent commits suicide?" Kerrie asked.

The mother didn't lift her head.

"Statistically," Kerrie continued, "they are more likely to take their lives."

The woman stared at her—a mother's love kicking in.

Kerrie told Tara about that case one evening. "She turned her life around."

Kerrie represented hundreds of suicidal patients, helping them realize they had good reason to soldier on.

"How's Willa doing out there?" Kerrie continued. Willa had reluctantly followed her husband's career to a far-away state. Kerrie laughed, thinking of how proud Willa had been of one of Kerrie's accomplishments the last time they'd been together.

"Getting divorced," Tara said. "She's staying out there for her daughter."

Neither knew as they talked that Willa lay dead. Hours earlier, she'd taken her life.

Kerrie sat through the funeral thinking of their indomitable grandmothers, wondering what could have made a difference. Willa had always carried a photo of her daughter. Kerrie thought if Willa could have just realized the impact it would have on her child, Willa wouldn't have taken her life. If she had written on that photo, *My daughter will do what I do*, it might have changed everything.

Both women wished Willa had come home.

If you're thinking of taking your life, go and be with someone you love. Really consider the impact it will have on your children, your parents, your siblings, and your grandparents. Call or text the suicide hotline:

1-800-273-TALK OR Text 741741.

They're available 24/7, and the call is confidential.

What to expect when texting a suicide hotline:

If you have never contacted a suicide hotline, here's exactly what happens. We sent a text to 741741.

1:53 p.m. our text: "Is this the text hotline?"

1:53 p.m. response: "Thanks for texting Crisis Text Line, where you'll text with a compassionate Crisis Counselor...what's on your mind?"

1:54 p.m. text: "Just wanted to see if the number worked."

1:54 p.m. response: "We're getting a crisis counselor for you, it may take a moment."

1:56 p.m. response: "Thanks for texting...we're 100% real! A group of trained counselors." (She then responded to our questions.)

What to expect when calling a suicide hotline:

Never called a suicide hotline? We did today. 1-800-273-TALK

A friendly young woman answered within a minute and said, "What's going on?" She was ready to help with whatever problem I had.

I explained that I was writing a column and asked whether worried friends and family could also contact them.

"Definitely!" she said.

If you suspect someone has lost hope, intervene. Friends and family can call these numbers. Do that now. Get help today.

We each need to pay attention. Scripture says: "Do not merely look out for your own personal interests, but also for the interests of others."[43]

You never know what another person is going through.

[43] Philippians 2:4 (NASB)

-13-

Billy Graham

Take It to the Lord In Prayer

"…do not be anxious about anything, but in everything by prayer and supplication, with thanksgiving, let your requests be made known to God. And the peace of God, which surpasses all understanding, will guard your hearts and your minds in Christ Jesus."

PHILIPPIANS 4:6[1]

[1] ESV

Take It to the Lord In Prayer

I've seen her several times in a store where I shop. She's hard to miss, always smiling, always a kind word for the workers there. I noticed her the other day as she stopped before entering the place, saw her eyeing a man in the parking lot. Suddenly it seemed as though a gale of sorrow swept over her.

She kept moving forward, her head down now, but clearly she'd been reminded of something unpleasant. One of the store's workers approached her as she stepped inside.

"Are you okay?" he asked.

I watched as she lifted her head and forced a smile. "Yes. Why?"

He hesitated, studying her. "You look so unhappy."

She shook her head. "It's nothing prayer can't fix."

I smiled. Her words reminded me of Billy Graham's favorite hymn. Here's how it goes:

What a friend we have in Jesus,
all our sins and griefs to bear!
What a privilege to carry
everything to God in prayer!
O, what peace we often forfeit,

O, what needless pain we bear,
all because we do not carry
everything to God in prayer.

Powerful!

That same day I overheard two people talking, a woman trying to help a man who seemed as though he was sinking

"I believe," she said, "that God is the answer to all problems."

It's true. God will show you the right path and strengthen you on your way. He will comfort you in time of trouble. If you need a miracle, He is the God of miracles.

Listen to what happens when Paul and his disciple are visiting the early Christian churches. They're beaten in a marketplace and then thrown into jail.

At midnight, the other prisoners suddenly hear the two praying and singing hymns. Immediately, there's an earthquake—the prison doors are thrown open and all shackles are broken. The jailer, certain they've escaped and knowing it means death for him, draws his sword to take his life.

"Don't harm yourself!" Paul shouts. "We are all here!"

Paul will lead the jailer and his family to Jesus that night. The jailer will care for the two in his home, binding their wounds, then return them to the prison.

At daylight, the magistrates send word to release Paul and his disciple, but Paul won't go. He's indignant, claiming the judges have unjustly imprisoned and beaten them.

When the magistrates hear this and discover that Paul is a Roman citizen, they fearfully bury their pride. These judges come to the jail and apologize.[2]

Look at our God in action: What seemed a desperate situation turned into salvation for the jailer and victory for God!

I saw that prayerful woman from the store this past weekend, and she shared some of her life with me. She knows hardship, as did Paul in prison. We all do. Everyone needs help.

She went on to tell me about her devotional life.

"Sometimes," she said, "God reaches out and shows me a person in a wheelchair or with cancer. Seeing their terrible misfortune changes everything. Immediately, it blots out any discouragement I feel. I lift my heart and give thanks for all that God has given to me."

I nodded. I've had that experience.

"At other times," she continued, "it takes a while to pray through my pain. God always sends an answer—maybe from another person, or sometimes I simply feel His guidance. Music really helps me."

"What kind of music?"

"Hymns."

I grinned, thinking of Paul singing hymns in prison, and how Jesus and the disciples sang a hymn after the Last Supper.

"Which ones do you like?" I asked.

She thought a moment. "I love *Be Still My Soul*, but my favorite is *What a Friend We Have in Jesus.*"

Ding-ding-ding!

---

[2] Acts16:16-40

If you have forgotten all the words, go online to YouTube. You'll be surprised to see how many mega stars have recorded this song. Like Billy Graham, they proudly sing of what they do when life gets rough: Take it to the Lord in prayer.[3]

---

[3] "What A Friend We Have In Jesus" was written by Joseph Scriven (1820-1886).

-14-

TAMAR

"YEP, THAT WAS ONE BIG WOOPSIE DOODLES!"

"…Judah begat Perez and Zerah, whose mother was Tamar…"

MATTHEW 1:3[4]

[4] NIV & KJV, together

"Yep, that was one big woopsie doodles!"

Woopsie doodles—urban slang for a big mistake.

Early one morning, my friend Jane painstakingly made a beautiful cheese soufflé. She had just sat down to eat when Penny, her coonhound, hastened to the table.

"You're not getting any," Jane said.

The big red dog stared at the soufflé.

"Go away," she continued.

Penny immediately eyed a bag of cookies, grabbed them, raced across the kitchen, out the dog door, and up a steep hill behind the house. Now, my very bright dog would have promptly ripped that bag open and downed every one of those cookies. But Penny was different. She deserved a place in Mensa.

Once Jane scaled the hillside, Penny politely handed over the bag of baked goods.

"Nice dog!" she said.

Penny grinned, galloped down the hill, raced through the house, and devoured one beautiful cheese soufflé.

Jane said she stared at the swinging dog door, mouth hanging open, knowing she'd just been had by a coonhound.

That's a true woopsie doodles.

Tamar is one of the best woopsie doodles in the Bible. This story is a little bit steamy—okay, it's a lot steamy—so cover your kids' eyes.

Tamar is mentioned in what I call *The Begats*, which open the New Testament—Abraham begat Isaac, Isaac begat Jacob, Jacob begat Judah and so on. It's the ancestry.com for our Lord, tracking a span of 2,000 years from Abraham to Joseph and then Jesus.

Boring stuff, right?

Hardly—just you wait and see!

Judah, fourth generation in the genealogy, marries and has three sons. His eldest son weds Tamar, then dies without an heir.

It was the duty of a brother-in-law to keep his brother's line alive, so Judah's second son marries Tamar. He also dies, also without a child.

Judah then tells Tamar to go to her father's house in another town and to live as a widow. He promises to let her wed his youngest son when the boy is of age.

Tamar agrees.

Years later, when the boy grows up, Judah's true intention becomes clear. He thinks the woman is a curse and isn't about to lose his last son to her.

Tamar realizes the promise will never be met. She knows that leaves her without an heir.

More time passes and Judah's wife dies (kids' eyes covered, right?). He's struck with grief but eventually returns to work. Tamar hears he will be passing by her town and devises a bold plan. She quickly sheds her widow's clothes, wears a veil to disguise herself, and poses as a prostitute.

Judah sees this woman in her veils and comes over to her. I'll let the Bible continue the story:

"Come, now, let me sleep with you," he says.

"What will you give me to sleep with you?" she asks.

"I'll send a goat from my flock."

"Will you give me something as a pledge until you send it?"[5]

He leaves his carved staff and several other items, all distinctive to him. He then returns home and sends the goat. But the woman can't be found.

"We have no town prostitute," the people there tell him.

Months later, Judah is informed that Tamar has played the harlot and is pregnant. He's furious.

"Bring her out and burn her!" he shouts.

She immediately sends a message to her father-in-law with the things she had taken as a pledge.

"I'm pregnant by the man who owns these," she says.

Of course he recognizes them. Judah also knows he's cheated her out of his third son and the possibility of an heir.

"She's in the right," he says. "I'm in the wrong."

Tamar bears twins and her first child will become the great, great, great, (add many more great's) grandfather of Jesus. See how Tamar ends up in *The Begats*. Old Testament prophecy says the Messiah will descend from the tribe of Judah, but without Tamar that might not have happened. In fact, there might not have been a tribe of Judah among the 12 tribes of Israel. Imagine that.

---

[5] Gen. 38: 16-17 NIV

The next time you read through Jesus' ancestry, hopefully you will think of the lives of these men, and a few remarkable women. They were real people. Some had truly interesting and important stories—one quite saucy. In fact, when you see Judah and Tamar listed there, you may recall their lives and say:

"Yep, that was one big woopsie doodles!"[6]

[6] The Scripture quotations in this section were taken from the NIV translation of the Holy Bible.

-15-

TIGLATH-PILESER IV

FIVE WORDS

"The Lord is close to the brokenhearted…"

PSALM 34:18[7]

[7] NIV

Five Words

If you approach my house from the rear street, before reaching the yard you can see through the trees to my back door. Normally, I don't pay attention. I've never actually stopped and searched through those trees—not until this past week.

Now I care.

As soon as I reach the trees, my heart fills with hope. I stop my vehicle and hastily scan the area. Just as quickly, sadness darkens my expectation. He's not there.

Tiglath-Pileser IV, my eight-month-old kitten, has been missing for the past week. It feels like months. He's solid black, neutered.

The first night, I suspected something very wrong had happened—I know my pet. Tiglath kept a Ronald Reagan presidential routine: up at five, returning midday for a nap, back at nine for bedtime.

Friends assured me he'd return. "He's off with his buddies," one said.

Except his feline pals still arrive each morning, looking for him. Less often, now.

The first night I was out at two in the morning, searching a wide radius around my house, certain I'd find him dead in the street. That didn't happen, thankfully.

But something got him.

I'm a live-and-let-live kind of person. I wonder now if I should have been more cautious. Something had tunneled into my yard, and I wonder if that something got him. Friday, for the first time in my life, I had pest control come. They took charge of that hole.

You learn in seminary that one death raises another. I found myself thinking of my parents this week. I sat in my car crying yesterday, uncertain just who I was grieving for. My kitten, yes—but also for those I've dearly loved and lost.

I wanted to write about sorrow months ago. My friend of three decades had called to tell me of her dad passing. He'd had a stroke and had been severely disabled for years. Her mom—this strong, devout, amazing woman—had cared for him all that time. She's one of a kind.

The funeral was on the West Coast, and I called the next morning. "I hope your dad's service went well."

"It was beautiful," she said, "but my mom passed in her sleep in the night."

As I write this, I can hear her weeping—something I'd never heard before. She's blonde with a sunny disposition. Her tears were the sound of clean, pure grief.

I'm well educated, but I never know what to say. At some point, I shared words I hold dear: "The Lord is close to the brokenhearted..."

I wanted to write something for her, but I told another friend, "All I can think of is the obvious."

Yesterday, as I was grieving, this second friend said, "The Lord is your shepherd."

Five words.

And the "obvious" brought me so much comfort.

If you are a person of faith, you'll know what that Psalm says:

The Lord is my shepherd, I shall not want.

He makes me lie down in green pastures.

He leads me beside still waters.

He restores my soul.

I found myself adding Jesus' words:

...my peace I give to you...

Come to Me, all who are weary and heavy-laden, and I will give you rest.

Loss can affect one deeply—it's readjusting your life to the void. If you love profoundly, it takes time. The larger the abyss, the longer it may be.

Norman Vincent Peale said to memorize Scripture, that it would bubble up and care for you in time of need. It will.

The Lord is your shepherd. He is close to the brokenhearted.[8]

---

[8] The Scripture quotations in this section were taken from the following versions of the Holy Bible: Psalm 34:8 (NIV), Psalm 23:1-3 (ESV), John 14:27 (ESV), Matthew 11:28 (NASB), respectively.

- 16 -

HEBREWS

BSB TIME

"…let us run with endurance the race that is set before us…"

HEB. 12:1[52]

[52] ESV

BSB Time

The moon is high in the sky as they make their way through the darkness, shivering from the cold, navigating empty streets. Each moves silently toward a vacant room in the basement of a large building. They have come for decades—one day each week. None has ever left this group, except by death.

They are not alone.

Many such groups meet elsewhere. They quietly gather, unbeknownst to most. They talk of blood and human sacrifice.

I know for a fact there's such a group in my town. Ten men.

Yes.

I knew one of them. Actually, I knew him pretty well. I had suspected he might be involved in such a matter—didn't know for sure.

On a fateful day, months ago, this man called me over to his table at lunch. Another man sat there.

Innocently, I joined them, never expecting what was about to happen.

He quietly introduced the other man, told me about their meetings, asked whether I'd come.

Obviously, I had an easy out: That time of day would be impossible.

But, oh no. Forget that. I decided to go.

Days later, I stumbled from my house into blackness—a full moon high in the sky—and braved those cold, dark, empty streets.

At a quarter before six in the morning, I stepped inside that basement.

What group?

I told this story to several people, wondering what they'd think.

"Witches," the first replied.

"No," another said. "The KKK."

It's my Bible study.

This account is how Romans and Jews saw the early Christian church. What we easily understand as communion and Christ's crucifixion, they thought were rituals of drinking blood and sacrificing humans. Such confusion contributed to hostility and persecution against the early church. Some Christians—faced with losing their property, homes, and even their lives—fearfully decided to leave the risen Lord.

The book of Hebrews addressed this crisis, emphasizing the importance of joining together: "Consider how we may spur one another on...not giving up meeting together...but encouraging one another." Heb. 10:24-25 (NIV)

This need is as strong today as ever. We face enormous pressure to "get with the times" and leave the commandments of God. Every Christian should attend church and find a small Bible study. We are stronger together.

When I walked into that church basement, my friend wasn't there to introduce me. Only a few men had arrived—they sat at a table for ten. I recognized one and smiled, maybe with a wave, I can't remember.

Obviously, I was faced with "group dynamics"—yes, you do know what I mean. Imagine showing up for church and another family having taken your pew.

"We thought we'd change it up," they say.

You stand there nodding with your mouth hanging open, wanting to say, "It's MY pew!"

Group dynamics.

This pre-crack-of-dawn Bible study had met for decades. Clearly, each man had his seat.

If I'd been alert, I'd have asked where to sit. But, no, my brain moves on turtle legs at a quarter 'til six—inching along.

I just sat down.

I didn't know at the time that one of the ten often couldn't attend. What are the odds I'd pick his seat? Ten to one, right? Ten percent chance.

Now add in the possibility I'd also pick the seat beside my thoughtful friend, who still hadn't arrived. I'm guessing less than one percent.

Obviously, that couldn't happen. I sat in someone else's seat, right? Must have.

And the Lord sayeth, "Oh, snap!"

I chose the oft-vacant seat, and it's right beside my friend's!

Impossible odds.

God was saying, "This is where you belong!"

Our Lord is always talking to us—through people, Scripture, and incidents like this. Perhaps even right now, as you read these words.

Join a small Bible study. You'll love your BSB's—Bible Study Buddies. These folk will be with you in sorrow and joy.

A friend of mine treasures her Bible study group saying, "A wonderful benefit is the relationships you develop...getting a group who will pray for you. These are the people I emailed from the hospital when my dad was dying."

My BSB's strengthen me in my walk with Jesus. "Iron sharpens iron..."[53]

We all need these things.

Scripture tells us plainly: "...lay aside every encumbrance and the sin which so easily entangles us, and let us run with endurance the race that is set before us." [54]

Yes, BSB's should be a part of every Christian's life.

[53] Proverbs 27:17 (NASB)

[54] Hebrews 12:1 (NASB)

- 17 -

BARTIMAEUS

WHAT GOD PLACES ON YOUR HEART

"God has not given us a spirit of fear… but of power…"

2 TIM. 1:7[55]

[55] NLT

What God Places On Your Heart

Elizabeth was five years old when she destroyed her mother. Elizabeth, the youngest of nine children, knew whose turn it was to say grace. It didn't matter that her mother had invited the preacher and his wife for dinner, it was still her turn.

She displayed great reverence, her hands folded in prayer on her plate, her chubby legs dangling quietly beneath the table.

"Jesus, thank you for this food!" she stated loudly.

The preacher, thinking the child had finished, eyed her mother, nodding his approval.

"And, Jesus," Elizabeth continued, "please don't bless nobody but us!"

Elizabeth's "me and mine" stage was corrected quickly. Her mother earnestly believed in generosity toward others.

Jesus also confronts "me and mine" selfishness as He's leaving Jericho one day. Surrounded by a great crowd moving along with Him, Jesus abruptly stops and says, "Call him here."

Call whom?

Jesus doesn't say, but the crowd knows.

Blind Bartimaeus had been sitting by the road, listening closely as the throng approached. Realizing it's the Lord, he shouts, "Jesus, son of David, have mercy on me!"

The whole crowd must have been clamoring for Jesus' attention, but Jesus focuses on this blind man. Why? Perhaps because Bartimaeus had become a spectacle—there wasn't just one in the crowd trying to silence him, Scripture says there were "many."

It gets worse.

Every version of this story I've read is almost identical, but at this place in the narrative they diverge. The New American Standard says the silencers spoke "sternly" to Bartimaeus. Another version says they "rebuked" the man. A third says they *warned him*.

Warned him?

Were people threatening this blind man for yelling to Jesus? Did he face a beating if he didn't quiet down?

What else can a warning mean?

The threats don't stop him.

Bartimaeus yells louder, begging Jesus for help. And a sizeable number of people in that crowd keep trying to stop him. A spectacle, as I said.

But why?

The Bible abounds with people bringing the sick and handicapped to Jesus. Why didn't someone help Bartimaeus through the crowd to Jesus?

Maybe the other healings were the "me and mine" kind—my family, my servants.

Bartimaeus was alone.

A beggar.

The "me and mine" folk weren't about to let him get ahead of them.

It's painful to read, much less to have experienced.

Our Lord says, "Call him."

I love this part. Love it!

Jesus doesn't go to the man or send the disciples for him. Usually He did one or the other, right?

Instead, Jesus speaks to the crowd. Deliberately.

Our Lord says, "Call him here."

You know what that means.

Those closest to Bartimaeus, the "me and mine" folk, must tell the blind man that the Lord wants him.

Blind Bartimaeus was not otherwise handicapped, nor was he an old man. Scripture says Bartimaeus jumps to his feet upon hearing Jesus' words.

Even so, how can this blind man get through the crowd to Jesus?

Watch me grin. I bet those beside the blind beggar, the ones threatening him, are now forced to lead him to Jesus.

"What do you want me to do for you?" Jesus asks Bartimaeus.

"Rabbi, I want to see," he says.

Jesus heals him immediately. "Go, your faith has made you well."

When Jesus was in His hometown, He couldn't perform many miracles because the people didn't believe.

Bartimaeus believed.

Even so, if Bartimaeus hadn't kept shouting, if he'd given up, Bartimaeus would have lived and died a blind beggar. But Bartimaeus kept shouting and shouting, fighting to get our Lord's attention.

Do the same. Do not give up!

Jesus shamed the crowd that day, but know that those people live on. They'll fight you, trying to instill fear in you as they did with Bartimaeus. You aren't going to get ahead of them, not if they can help it. They act from selfishness, rivalry, jealousy.

Don't listen to them.

The biggest naysayer may be yourself, thinking you aren't good enough for the new opportunity, the new house, the new relationship. We shush our yearning and walk away, refusing to try.

"No one is going to publish this," I said after writing my first newspaper article.

Had it been left to me, I'd have thrown it away. But I'd promised someone, so I submitted that article. Then my first editor, Jay Thomas, published it and kept publishing my pieces, believing in me. Otherwise, I would not have become a faith columnist.

As I edit this in 2017, most newspapers do not want words about Jesus. Thankfully, I was guided to one that did.

If God places something on your heart, seize the opportunities that come. You disappoint Him if you say, "I can't—"

Let me repeat that: You disappoint God if you say, "I can't—"

Little Elizabeth's "me and mine" self-centeredness and the crowd's selfishness were both quickly corrected. Bartimaeus received healing because of his faith, but also because he kept yelling to Jesus.

Be as strong as Bartimaeus.

"God has not given us a spirit of fear...but of power..." 2Tim. 1:7[56]

---

[56] The Scripture quotations in this section were taken from the following translations of the Holy Bible: Mk. 10:49 (NASB), Mk. 10:47 (NASB), Mk. 10:47 (NASB), Mk. 10:49 (NASB), Mk. 10:49 (NASB), Mk. 10:51 (NIV), Mk. 10:52 (NASB), and 2Tim. 1:7 (NLT), respectively.

PART II

Guidance From God

-18-

STRANDED IN THE DEEP SOUTH

Author's note:

This is the first article I wrote for a newspaper. Before this, I had won four local writing awards and had been asked to enter a newspaper column-writing contest. Honestly, it didn't interest me.

I wrote this article because someone I owed a favor insisted that I do it. I had no expectation my thoughts would be published. As you will see, this selection is a lot longer than others in the book—I didn't know the correct length for a newspaper article.

I take seriously the words of Proverbs 11:14: "...in the abundance of counselors there is victory."[57] In other words, I really listen to my editors. However, they were at opposite ends of the spectrum on this article. Some loved every word and wanted me to leave it completely intact, while others felt it needed to be shorter. I did edit it heavily from the original, but it's still a good deal longer than the rest of the chapters.

[57] NASB

"My Presence will go with you, and I will give you rest."

EXODUS 33:14[58]

[58] NIV

Stranded in the Deep South

When a woman starts a 1,000 mile road trip, she thinks of Ted Bundy or those Cleveland women held in captivity. The Friday before Memorial Day in 2015, I began just such a trip from deep in the South, heading north. I wasn't sure how long I'd be gone—I packed winter clothes, if that gives you any idea.

I have two vehicles: A Cadillac with 100,000 miles and a Jeep with 250,000 miles. Obviously, the Cadillac was the better choice. Obviously.

I had taken it to my local mechanic who had given me the thumbs up. Even so, as I drove north, that vehicle started talking to me and not in a good way. It was sick. It sputtered.

Okay, but just how sick are you?

I kept going, hoping she was overreacting. It was just the sniffles, a cold starting for a few of the two hundred horses under her hood. Before long, the engine began fighting me—it had a fever. Something very serious was going on.

Stubborn, I kept going, certain it wasn't that serious, certain the mechanic would have known, certain he wouldn't have let me start on this trip in an unsafe vehicle.

Finally, it threatened to die, over and over again. The engine was not getting fuel, or at least it felt like that. I looked at my mileage indicator—I had driven less than 100 miles, how could this be happening?

I pulled off the road at the first station and started hearing beeping. Was this my vehicle? It now sounded like a bomb about to explode. I looked around and frowned. It seemed as though it was the station, but that was crazy—gas stations don't beep.

"Out of business!" a man yelled from the house next door. Apparently the beeping had something to do with the station's status.

It was probably the hottest day of the year, and he sat back in the shadows of his garage. I walked toward him gingerly, hoping he wasn't related to Ted. Bundy, that is.

I explained about the car trouble, eyeing his small "Boiled Peanuts" sign.

Seriously? The hottest day of the year?

Then I turned and eyed the road. Cleary, the man had more than one problem. His house sat way back from the highway—anyone passing at a clip wouldn't have noticed him or his house, much less his little sign.

"Just go down to the Texaco," he said. "Best mechanic in town!"

He gave me long, detailed directions.

"Okay," I said, paying no attention. How big could this little town be?

At the first light, I realized the city was a bit larger than I had anticipated. I remembered him saying something about a hill, and a light, and the left side of the road. I turned the corner and searched.

No hill. No Texaco, left or right.

I wandered around in circles then stopped and asked again.

"You passed it," the next man said. "Best mechanic in town. Right there!"

So I backtracked, paying a lot more attention to the second set of directions.

No Texaco.

I stopped again. "Where EXACTLY is it?"

I followed those directions to a tee. No Texaco. I did see a "Service Center" and eyed the tower in front as I pulled in. It looked like it might have once been a sign.

"Is this the Texaco?" I asked.

"Used to be," the man said.

I smiled. *No, sir, it still is.*

The first mechanic, who'd given me the thumbs up, had also put in a new compressor, new hose, and new Freon. So at least I had just driven those 100 miles on the hottest day of the year in a cool vehicle. Right?

Wrong.

The air didn't work either. I retreated inside the service center, sweating profusely—that area was cooler than outside. A man followed after me and turned on a window air conditioner.

Did I look that bad? Probably.

A nice woman asked if I needed an appointment for next week.

"I'm not going to be here next week," I said, alarm in my voice. "I'm just passing through headed north. Can someone look at my vehicle now?"

Everyone dropped everything and came to my aide. I was grateful. Even more grateful to be in the hands of the "best mechanic in town." That was the unanimous opinion on my pilgrimage to the not-Texaco. No better mechanic anywhere.

The best mechanic in town didn't take long to return. Something about a torque—I didn't pay attention. What I heard was the part about him not being able to fix it.

You're kidding? The best mechanic in town? You can't fix it?

He sent me down the road to another place, saying he took his vehicle there. Okay, I really, really liked that part. I am now off to the best-mechanic-in-town's mechanic. Good hands, right?

I listened closely to the directions and followed them to a tee. No sign anywhere. I did see several large garages and a smaller building with many vehicles parked outside.

Is this the place?

There wasn't a soul in sight.

I got out, swiping at sweat on my brow. Why did I think there would be a sign—some words somewhere that mentioned Automotive Repair? Why did I think that?

I walked toward the buildings gingerly.

Anybody in captivity in there?

You never know.

Fairly quickly, a man emerged from the garage. He seemed safe enough, so I recounted my tale—the engine fighting me, the not-Texaco guy saying something about a torque, the 1,000 mile trip. He said there was no way he could fix it, that he'd be working late finishing what he had on hand. He told me no one was going to be open anywhere on Memorial Day weekend.

"If you find a place," he continued. "You wouldn't want them working on your car."

The man didn't look like a sage, but there was truth in those words. He said he wasn't coming back to work until Tuesday.

"Can you please just look at it?" I asked.

"No."

"You can't even tell me if you can fix it on Tuesday? I don't want to wait four days if you can't fix it."

"No."

He gave me a reason, something about codes and this and that. I couldn't listen—all I could think about was being stranded in a tiny Southern town for four whole days. Worse yet, the acute realization hit me that on Tuesday morning the best-mechanic-in-town's mechanic might not be able to fix my vehicle. Actually, I'm pretty sure he said this.

"You could go to Enterprise," he added.

"You want me to rent a car?"

"Enterprise is a city."

I made a very fast executive decision—for me, this is quite rare. I didn't know anyone in Enterprise, and it was far away. I wasn't even certain I could get there. This guy already had more recommendations than anyone I could possibly find in such a short space of time. I wanted him.

"Tuesday," I said. "I'll be back."

I drove around the corner and checked into the local hotel. The rate gagged me.

You get that here?

The woman smiled and made me a better deal.

It's dinner time now (what the deep South calls *supper*. Good thing we drifted to this topic because that can cause you trouble. Like when someone says, "Come by after dinner," and you go at six p.m., but they expected you after lunch.)

I returned to the downtown area to the only people I know—my new besties at the not-Texaco. I pulled out my credit card to get gas. No slot. I went inside.

"How much do you want?" she asked.

"I have no idea." I waived the credit card midair. "There's always a slot."

She nodded toward the pump, the pump closest to the road. "Just go ahead and get it."

Seriously?

So I did, wondering when I'd last bought gas without paying for it first. Gas by the road, no less. Well, let's see—not in this decade, probably not in this century.

I returned and handed her my card, still sweating.

"All set!" I said, proud of adjusting so quickly to small-town living.

"How much did you get?"

I stared at her. *I'm supposed to know this?*

Before I could reach for the door, her husband dashed outside and right back with the amount. Talk about a man with energy!

They gave me a list of the local eating establishments, pointing this way and that. I wrote down the names, wondering if any of them would have a sign.

What does one do on a long weekend in a little Southern town while waiting on car repairs? I found out. I went and looked at the lake. Nice lake. The part about the island and a picnic sounded wonderful—that is until the man at the gate mentioned the eleven alligators.

"They won't hurt you," he said.

I knew why he added that part. I get a certain look when I think of Ted Bundy or the Cleveland women. Sheer fear. I'll call it my 11-alligator look.

"There was that one time . . ." he continued, his voice trailing off.

"What one time?"

"No one got hurt."

"What one time?"

"A man was swimming," he said, "and an alligator chased him, but he didn't bite him or anything."

Or anything? That's supposed to make me feel better!

I kept thinking about those eleven wise alligators eating people whole—no witnesses, no evidence.

The island picnic was a definite no.

I actually tried to get to a larger, nearby town, but the car threatened to die over and over again.

Fortunately, I do carry every manner of electronic gadget and worked part of the weekend. I tried several restaurants. The Italian place at the far end of town uses garlic in the most indecent fashion. Deliciously! I went to the grocery where I found the best peaches ever.

You have to remember this was supposed to be a two-day trip. My vehicle was packed to the gills for my indefinite stay up North. I had left out two sundresses, which was all I thought I needed. Did I want to go digging through my car for clothes? No. So I wore those two dresses. I didn't know anyone in town—what difference did it make?

Where I was living at the time, everyone dressed just like I do. I didn't see one sundress in this town. No one looked anything like I do. Just as an aside, everyone I met goes to church, just like I do. That's amazing. Simply amazing!

For reasons I cannot explain, I started looking at the real estate listings online. I like interesting, historic homes and eyed three. When I was out wandering around, I suddenly heard myself say, "If I could find a house with this one rare feature, I might buy it." After all, I wasn't far from where I lived. I could escape the summer craziness and save all my precious belongings from hurricanes.

As I roamed around, I passed all three of those houses. This was also amazing. I couldn't quite believe that every house online was right there, blocks apart.

Okay, fair to say I wasn't used to small-town living. At all.

Get ready for this: Lo and behold, one of the three houses had that rare feature I wanted!

I stopped my car and stared.

Not possible!

Was it fate? Synchronicity? God? What? I mean, what are the chances?

When you find such a rare feature, those homes are never for sale.

I got out of my car and approached the house, unsure if it was occupied. One would hate to get caught peeking into the windows where a person lives—I'm also pretty certain it's a crime. I kept circling the house on foot, moving closer and closer until I was sure it was empty. Then I peered into one room after another, nose to the glass.

What a charming, old house!

It's now the Sunday before Memorial Day, and I called a close friend and told him about the house.

"Have you lost your marbles!" he shouted. "You cannot stop in a little town and buy a house!"

That did not dissuade me. I explained how I really hated the idea of keeping my grandmother's prayer table on a barrier island.

"No, No, No!" he continued. "NO!"

I went back and looked at the house.

The man across the street was an unbelievable sign. (I love signs and wonders—I live for them.) He's not only the associate minister at the Baptist church, he also has the most gorgeous yard. And I'm not even at the unbelievable part. Not yet. Here it comes: My dog, Baby, decided his yard, with him standing there watching, was the best place in the world to poop.

"I'll get that!" I quickly said, having been scolded more than once for Baby's poor judgment.

"It's good for the ground," he said.

"It is?" I grinned. *Yes, I want you for my neighbor!*

He directed me to the next block down, telling me about Ms. Libby.

"It was her parent's house," he said. "She knows all about it."

I trooped right down there. Even so, I knew not everyone wants their day interrupted by an enthused, adventurous soul. Right away, I saw the sign by the door and felt certain I was in good hands. It read, "As for me and my house, we shall serve the Lord."

I rang the doorbell and a woman appeared, looking at me quizzically.

"Are you Ms. Libby?" I asked.

Immediately, the biggest smile imaginable filled her face. "I am."

She and her husband settled into the porch swing and told me all about the charming, old house.

Did I mention this part—I love the people in this little town!

"I'm going to take you to church with us," her husband said.

I have lived in my much-larger town many years, and no one has ever invited me to church. Not once. Nada.

I actually took one of my electronic gadgets and listened to their minister. Isn't the electronic age something? You can go back in time and listen to a sermon that happened weeks ago in your hotel room with a few taps of a finger.

I liked what he had to say. My grandmother was a minister, I was raised by the daughter of a minister—I could go on and on. Unlike my listening skills with mechanics, I pay attention to ministers. I know what's what, and he did a fine job.

David Ellis showed me the house on Memorial Day. I had nothing else to do. I feel certain he had plenty happening—a day scheduled to the max with family events. But I told him if, miracle of miracles, my car was ready to go on Tuesday morning, I was heading north immediately. I didn't want to go north at all, but there were things to do. Pressing things.

"This may be the only day I have to see it," I told David.

Remember, I have no a/c, and Baby was sick. I didn't want her in the heat, so I asked if we could go "early." Seven a.m. early.

We did. David Ellis proved to be the sweetest, most flexible, laid-back realtor ever—wonderful man!

As I drifted deeper and deeper into the house, I began doing the math.

"It needs some work," I said. "The expensive kind."

Actually, I said a lot more, but I'd bore you with the details.

I went to the local diner after that and asked if the town was a safe place to live. Of course, it is. I get that now, but on day three I had no idea. One of the waitresses actually knew the woman who had owned the house after Ms. Libby. Why does that not surprise me?

One of the locals recommended the restaurant's cheesecake. Uh, yes, the cheesecake is wonderful. I need to stay away from the diner.

On Tuesday, I was up at 5 a.m.—D-day for my car. I called what I thought was my mechanic and an elegant British woman on the voice recording asked me to leave a message.

What?

"Uh—" I said and stopped, certain I had the wrong number. I left a message anyway, reminding him of our conversation on Friday.

Immediately thereafter, I went by his place. Did he start at six? Seven?

No.

Also, no sign indicating hours of operation. I stuck a note under the door with my name and number, reminding him who I was.

I also called from breakfast at the diner. Yes, my mind was swirling, wondering if he would have time to diagnose it on Tuesday. He answered and told me to come at 9:30. I was there at 9:20. I am never early for anything. Never.

People came with their cars and sob stories—why did that all sound so familiar? Oh yes, they were just like me. He told them next week, patiently listening as they poured out their troubles.

The man underestimated his ability to decipher my problem. He knew within minutes and quickly made a phone call. I listened; it sounded dire. It was.

To paraphrase, my Cadillac was bad news back when it was birthed. He told me a lot of mechanical things which I didn't understand. The bottom line: Don't take it anywhere.

I have to take it. I have to get there!

"Can you make it better?" I said.

"Yes."

"Let's go with that."

He ordered some parts—estimated time of arrival Thursday. He also looked at the a/c and said there wasn't a drop of Freon in it. That didn't surprise me. He put in dye and coolant. Thankfully, I was cool again.

Something made me call him later that afternoon. Was it:

(a) Jesus;

(b) My guardian angel;

(c) The Holy Spirit or;

(d) All of the above?

I'm going with (d).

"I have another vehicle," I said. "It has a quarter of a million miles on it, so . . ."

I waited. Obviously he was going to tell me to forget it, to take the Cadillac.

He didn't miss a beat. "Anything would be better than that Cadillac."

Are you serious?

Honestly, I don't think I'd heard a word he'd said until that moment.

Enter the local Exxon. I had learned they would take me anywhere I wanted to go. After a flurry of phone calls with the man at Exxon, we decided to travel hours south and get the Jeep that afternoon.

"I'm on my way into the lot," the man finally said.

"I'm coming!" I grabbed my things and scurried out of the hotel.

No Exxon.

"Where are you?" I said, calling him back. "I thought you were in the lot."

"No, I said I was on my way out of the lot."

"Where are you now?"

"On my way out of the lot."

You gotta love small town life.

Exxon arrived with a humongous vehicle. I opened the door and stared up at the steep climb.

"Little old ladies can get in here," he said.

I nodded. *Okay, then. No little old lady is going to best me. Not today, anyway.*

I hoisted Baby into the seat, lifted my full-length sundress, and climbed those steep steps to where even the elderly can go.

"I saw you eating in the diner yesterday," Preston Boutwell said right off, before we'd even left the hotel lot. I looked down at my clothes and winced.

In this.

I had an awakening at that moment—in this town where everyone knew everyone else, I stood out. One and only one thing flashed across my mind: *I have to break out a suitcase!*

"Does the Jeep run?" he asked.

"Yes, but it needs new tires."

"I'll make you a good deal!"

I see. Preston owns Exxon.

When you travel four hours with a person, you get to know them. I told Preston my life story, and he told me his. We told jokes. We shared our joys and our tragedies. We talked about the Bible—my great love, as if you didn't know. His favorite character (other than Jesus) is Paul. Mine is David. He likes the Gospels the best. I love the Gospels, too. I also treasure the Old Testament, love those stories.

I warned him that my Jeep was in storage with boxes of junk all around it. I told him there were about five, and I'd have to stuff that stuff in the Jeep. I didn't want to pay a huge storage bill for a few boxes.

Fine with him.

When we arrived, it was obvious I had remembered this wrong—there were a lot more than five boxes.

Preston treated me like kin folk and grabbed one box after another, fishing stuff out and shoving it into that SUV. It was amazing. Believe me, not many people would have done that. It was also hot, really hot. We were both sweating, and I felt terrible, but he acted like it was absolutely nothing. It wore me out. Preston, who could retire if he wanted to, didn't look a bit scathed.

Preston has a son who works with him, younger Preston. Preston keeps in touch with people who go way back. He lives for football games and enjoys them with the same couples. He eats every morning with men from his church. He's lived in that little town all his life. I'd say he has a good life.

We dropped the Jeep to get it repaired, and I went by first thing on Wednesday morning and cleaned out enough stuff so a human could get inside. Yes, it was that full. Then I waited for the verdict from the best-mechanic-in-town's mechanic. I thought for certain I'd have to take the parts he'd ordered for the Cadillac (I'd already paid for them). But he had somehow cancelled that. He looked at the Jeep, called me, and was elated that he could make it all work for the same price he'd quoted me on the Cadillac.

Meanwhile, I have nothing to do for most of Wednesday and am circling that historic house. The police stopped twice and gave me a good once over. I loved that!

An interested police force is a great thing!

I called my friend back. "I'm going to make an offer."

"No, you're not!" he said. "No! No! NO!"

I made the offer.

On Thursday, I had to check out of the hotel at noon. My car wouldn't be ready until five, so I pretty much lounged around the auto place with nowhere else to go.

"Great location," I said.

He's right at the corner of three major highways. Inevitably the land will be in demand, and when that happens, he plans to sell and retire.

He's not an old man.

"What are you going to do when you retire?" I asked.

It didn't take him long to answer. "Open a little repair shop somewhere."

I couldn't help but smile. Isn't that the essence of contentment—to love what you're doing so much you'd continue if you had all the money in the world? I saw that in both Preston and David. They love what they do. Me too!

Of course, it had to storm that afternoon. At five, after transferring all my belongings from one vehicle to the other in the rain and mud, I hurried to the Exxon. I had already priced the tires for my Jeep, and Preston was good to his word—he made me a great deal. I rolled in and his men set to work like a well-oiled machine. I am not kidding! Fifteen minutes later I was rolling out!

Why were people so nice to me? Could it be I had simply landed in a nice town? It almost felt like these people came from that long-ago era when honor meant more than money. They knew I needed help and wanted to help me.

I finished my trip north Saturday night. Nice tires, nice ride.

Did the best-mechanic-in-town's mechanic keep me safe from the hands of the Ted Bundy's of the world? Definitely.

As for David Ellis—did I buy that house? Let me say these words from God: "My Presence will go with you, and I will give you rest."[59]

I made multiple offers for two months. All of them were refused. Next is a big-fish tale you must read to understand how the story ends. And it's regular length.[60]

---

[59] Ex. 33:14 NIV

- 19 -

THE ISRAELITES

A BIG-FISH TALE

"…do not forget the things your eyes have seen…"

DEUT. 4:9[61]

[61] NIV

A Big-Fish Tale

There are big-fish tales. You know what I mean, highly unlikely stories—the kind that cause old men to yell, "Balderdash!"

This is one of them.

Honestly, I wouldn't have the pluck to tell it, but there are witnesses. Living ones.

My big-fish tale begins the week before Memorial Day, when I was hurrying north on a dreaded road trip—the one I wrote about previously in chapter 18. My mother's red Cadillac decided to break down near a small town, and the best mechanic there waved me down the road to his mechanic. After a week of drama, I switched vehicles, then made the trip north safely in my Jeep.

Before I could leave, however, I had to transfer all my belongings from one vehicle to the other. Mind you, every day I'd spent in that little town had been hot and sunny, but now it started to storm. At five o'clock, quitting time, my mechanic stepped toward his garage door. By now I was soaked to the bone and still stuffing my Jeep. Even so, I saw him hesitate, glancing up at the door, then down toward the opening.

"Can I help you?" he asked, eyeing my totes, the ones that had somehow wandered inside his garage, making it impossible for him to go home.

"Yes." I was tired

He loaded the remaining items, shifting things so I could see.

I stepped back, grateful for the aid.

"I wish I could say this sort of thing never happens to me." I swiped at the rain dripping from my chin as mud squished over my sandals. "But it happens all the time."

"When I was eight," he said, shutting the door, "my mom told me I prayed to God for patience." He paused, then turned and moved away. "You shouldn't pray to God for patience."

"You shouldn't?" That was odd—patience is a fruit of the Spirit. I long to be more patient. "Why not?"

"Because," he said, "God will send you calamity."

Honestly, I looked around, wondering what he meant, then stopped abruptly.

He's talking about me!

There are people—professionals—who say there are no accidents. They insist that one brings disaster upon oneself. At moments like these, I tend to agree—I always think I'm at fault. Accordingly, I knew who to blame for my next episode of vehicular failure. It didn't help that this mechanic had said the Jeep would outlast me, that it could go 900,000 miles with regular service.

Not what happened.

I had been up North for about three weeks before returning home, deep in the South.

Did my Jeep die in any of the half dozen states I had passed through? Did it die anywhere on those

1,000 miles of interstate I traveled? Did it quit near the little town where I had been stranded a week?

No, but it did fail.

On June 30th, one month after my mom's Cadillac was given last rites, my Jeep died right there, in that same town.

"Balderdash!" you shout.

There are witnesses, I tell you. Living ones!

And the odds. Oh, the odds must be phenomenal. What are the chances I could ever be stranded in that small Southern town, ever in an entire lifetime? Much less twice, a month apart? Much less with a different vehicle?

As the carnival barker says, "Tighten your belts! This ride gets better!"

My Jeep didn't break down just anywhere in that town—not on Main Street, not on the highway leading out of town, not even within pushing distance of my automotive mechanic.

Where then?

Every story must have a drumroll, and this is where mine goes. Believe me, it's worth the wait.

My Jeep died at the front door of the automotive repair shop. The front door!

"Balderdash!" you shout.

There are witnesses, I tell you. Living ones!

On that unsuspecting morning, I was headed to see the newspaper editor. I stopped to ask my mechanic a quick question, leaving my Jeep running. As I hurried back toward it, rounding the autos on the lot, the Jeep exploded in a gigantic cloud of steam so thick I couldn't see any part of my vehicle. Nothing. At all. The whole Jeep up in "smoke."

The engine died and water gushed to the ground beneath it.

Honestly, I wouldn't be penning this now if I had been inside—I wouldn't be right for a long time.

I rushed back toward the garage. My mechanic lay full-body in the mouth of a mammoth truck.

"Water—" That was all I could say.

"Was the a/c on?" He hadn't heard the Jeep and kept working. "That's normal."

"Come." I still couldn't talk.

He glanced up at me from the engine. "I can't," he said. "Not right this minute."

But he came immediately, probably because of that look I get—the 11-alligator one.

The best-mechanic-in-town's mechanic knew what to do. He opened the hood and reached into the engine. A melon-sized part promptly fell into his hand.

"It's your steering," he said, in a slow drawl.

I stared at the part and swallowed hard—I had felt the steering wheel fighting me.

"It-it-it just started," I stammered, thinking of those folks who say there are no accidents. "I put steering fluid in it. I did!"

That was true—I had, but apparently not soon enough.

He didn't answer me. Of course, it was my fault, and I wanted to stomp my foot. I should have checked that fluid, but I never do, and nothing like this has ever happened before. I rely on oil changes to catch those problems.

Despite this calamity, by nature I am a grateful person. I told the explosion story around town that afternoon, and more than one person lamented my misfortune.

"Good fortune!" I corrected. "I could have been on the interstate. Imagine what might have happened!"

Indeed, several years ago a friend of mine on a motorcycle skidded to a stop on I-65 in the rain. His bike flew out from under him, and he landed on the pavement. A tractor trailer rolled over his head. A true and tragic story.

That could have been me. If my Jeep had exploded on the interstate, coming to a dead halt, a tractor trailer could have run right over me, crushing my Jeep like a tin can.

There was silence when I returned to see about my Jeep. My mechanic eyed me.

"I know," I said. "I should have carefully checked the steering fluid."

"It wasn't your fault," he said.

"It wasn't?"

"It was a bracket." He stopped and shook his head. "A stress fracture."

"What?"

The way I understand this, the metal had cracked.

"The odds of that—" He looked away.

Apparently, the odds of a stress fracture were even greater than the odds of it happening in that same small town, with a different vehicle, a month apart, and at his doorstep.

Oh, yes. I got the message. God was determined to keep me safe that last day of June and also Memorial Day weekend. I believe that. But consider these two separate auto failures, both in the same place (neither of them my fault, I must righteously add). Was this a sign? Was I supposed to live in this town?!

Three days earlier, I had told my realtor I'd decided against the charming, old house. I'd told him to make an offer on another house far away.

I promptly went to see him. We looked at the house again, and I made another offer.

Miracles happen every day. They happen to you and to me—our big-fish tales.

Is each one the hand of God guiding and directing us? I believe so. Moreover, I strive to hold these moments close. There's good reason.

Why did the Israelites wander for 40 years? Why were the people of God taken into captivity after the grand reigns of David and Solomon?

They lost faith.

In their fear, suffering, and pride they turned from God. They sought help and guidance elsewhere.

But how did that happen? How could those chosen by God have forgotten all the miracles Moses showed to Pharaoh—the locusts, the bloody water, the death of every first-born Egyptian male? How come no one shouted, "The Red Sea parted!"

How could they have left God?

It happened. They forgot.

One of the saddest themes of the Bible is how God's people turned away from Him. The verses are too numerous to count. Here's just a smattering: II Kings 17:7-19, Nehemiah 9:13-31, Psalm 78:5-64, Ezekiel 33:10-29. As I said, the verses are too numerous to count.

Each of us will go through hard times—one does not get through a lifetime without suffering. But it is the miracles, the unbelievable moments with God, the times when we see Him gently caring for us, confidently guiding us—they make all the difference.

They embolden us.

They make us raise our eyes to heaven. They remind us to fall to our knees.

Remember the big-fish tales. Remember yours, remember those in the Bible. Boldly tell them to your children, your best friends, strangers in humongous trucks who pick up your Jeep, maybe even write them down in a book.

Big-fish tales from God must be cherished. The Lord reminds us: "...do not forget the things your eyes have seen..."[62]

---

[62]Deut. 4:9 NIV

- 20 -

PRESTON BOUTWELL

MORE THAN FULL SERVICE

"You are the light of the world. A city on a hill cannot be hidden."

"In the same way, let your good deeds shine out for all to see, so that everyone will praise your heavenly Father."

MT. 5:14[63], 5:16[64]

[63] NIV

[64] NLT

More Than Full Service

He's a robust man with a friendly word for everyone. Stop at his service station and ask Preston Boutwell how he's doing.

"Never had a bad day in my life!" he'll say. You can count on it.

If you read chapter 18, you'll know Preston and I don't go way back—only to last Memorial Day when calamity brought us together. We spent hours towing my Jeep to town, my little dog curled up between us.

I've liked him ever since.

I didn't realize on that day just how important Preston would become to me.

I was unexpectedly stranded in his town for a solid week. Three months later I bought a home there. One of the reasons was to give my dog and myself some sanity. My house has a nice yard and dog-friendly neighbors, neither of which we had where we'd lived before.

As I said in chapter 18, the day I first looked at the house, Baby pooped in the minister's yard across the street. The minister was so very nice about it. Baby also took a hankering to visiting the house on the corner. "Visiting" isn't exactly the right word—she would step up onto their veranda and make herself at home. I made a point to ask these neighbors if it was okay.

"Sure," they said. They didn't mind. But I am fairly certain their scrambling cats had another point of view.

A stray feline took to following Baby. Granted my dog was really sick, going to the vet twice a week, so there wasn't much Baby could do about it. The cat would walk inches from Baby's tail. I have no idea why, maybe because he could. Anyway, it was funny—a tiny parade.

When the local police saw her toddling along in the middle of the street, they showed great restraint. I'd wave, running to get her, and they'd wave back.

Baby's health had not been good for some time and continued to deteriorate. By November, the vet started saying bad things—that putting her "to sleep" was coming. I knew he was wrong. On one particular weekend, Baby felt better. We went to the beach, and she ate a nice piece of chicken for breakfast and meat again for lunch. Getting her to eat anything substantial could become my goal for the day, so obviously I was relieved.

Now dogs, even those with permits, are not allowed on this beach at midday. However, I am a particularly lucky person. I count on this.

I had lived on that beach for years and knew how it was patrolled. The sheriff has to cover a good many miles several times a day—the odds were low that he would see us.

So we're good, right? Smart me chose the time he would be at lunch.

Five minutes after we settled into the sand, Baby on my lap, he rolled past in his truck. I held my breath, eyeing him.

Go on, don't stop. Look the other way. Don't see us.

He stopped. The deputy then craned his head backwards and frowned at me.

"Strictly speaking," I said, as sweetly as possible, "she isn't on the sand." I'm an attorney, I have a nice grasp on technicalities. I also know the value of a smile and beamed at the lawman.

"Doesn't matter," he said roughly.

I had been rocking Baby, and he eyed her frail body cradled against my breast. It must have touched him.

"You can stay," he said with a sigh. "Just stay put."

We had every intention of "staying put." Baby could stand, but by now she couldn't really walk.

Since we had permission to be there, I lay back against the sand and let her body rest on mine. The surf was gentle, the sky blue, the breeze tender—a glorious day.

That weekend was also one of the saddest for me. My little dog took a turn for the worse when we arrived home and died just before midnight.

I am grateful to God for the joy she brought to my life, grateful she outlived the expectations of vet medicine for years. Even more thankful that she passed quietly by the hand of God and not by an injection.

I am beyond grateful.

The next morning, I found Preston at the local diner—his familiar truck outside. He eats breakfast there with his buddies before he heads to work, sitting at what is affectionately called, "The Liar's Table."

I joined them, trying to stay calm, relating the tragedy. Before long, I began crying then sobbing.

"Can I hire one of your men?" I asked him. "To help me bury her."

I didn't know what he'd say. Clearly it was a big imposition, he needed his men to run the gas station. But I was beside myself with grief, and she'd been dead for almost ten hours. I feared her body would begin to smell, and the thought of letting that happen wounded me more deeply. I could feel almost a panic starting inside. There I was in a new city with no friends—I didn't know where to turn.

Preston didn't hesitate. "We'll be over there in a little bit."

He arrived with one of his men as promised. I had moved her into the living room—still in her bed, her body covered with a hand towel.

"Will you check her?" I asked Preston. "Check her to be sure."

I had sat with her those ten hours, and she hadn't moved, lying there covered in quiet stillness. Even so, I held out hope, remembering the one-in-a-bazillion person who had returned to life unexpectedly at the funeral home.

"Check her," I asked, waving him toward her bed. "Check her to be sure."

He did. Soberly.

Obviously I was desperate, but he acted like it was a legitimate request.

He raised then lowered the towel. "She's gone."

I lifted her bed and carried her to the yard.

Preston didn't have to come to my house—he could have sent any one of his men. Remember, that's what I had asked for. After all, Preston has his Exxon to run. But he knew I needed a lot more than help with my dog. Preston knew I needed someone to care for me.

That was probably the most difficult part of this favor—trying to comfort someone crying. You know what I mean. You want to share something helpful. You hope to be caring, but who knows what to say?

Preston looked down at me. "You're going to be lost without your dog."

That was exactly how I felt. Only one small sentence, but it comforted me—profoundly. Preston understood, and the fact that he understood was what I needed.

Preston's worker, Michael Piland, is a young and strong man. He dug a very good hole and then looked to his boss for approval.

Preston stepped forward, surveyed the grave, and pointed to one side.

"Square it off over there," he said.

Michael nodded. Obviously this was important, it had to be right.

I clasped the bed tightly with Baby resting there, wanting to place her in the grave myself, but it was deeper than I could reach. Michael took her from me gingerly, as though he was lifting his own newborn. Carefully, he settled Baby into her final resting place.

He lifted the first shovel of dirt, placing it gently at the far end of her bed away from where her head lay beneath the towel. Fresh tears filled my eyes—it was a great kindness. He is a sensitive person. If he'd thrown dirt in there, I think my heart would have broken.

I couldn't watch as he lifted the second shovel of dirt into the grave. This part was too final. I retreated to a wall by the edge of my house.

Preston remained as his man finished closing the grave, carefully overseeing the final segment of the job. I tried to pay him, but Preston wouldn't take anything for her burial.

Jay Thomas, my first editor, told me how Preston had helped him, towing his vehicle.

"He didn't charge me anything," Jay said.

Preston has "Jesus Saves" on the side of his Exxon trucks. It's been a year now since Baby died, and I recently learned the story behind that message. He bought his first truck from a man who had "Jesus Saves" painted on it. A man offered to paint over it.

"Let me put the name of your business there," the man said.

"That is my business," Preston answered, knowing everything comes from God.

Jesus said: "You are the light of the world. A city on a hill cannot be hidden...In the same way, let your good deeds shine out for all to see, so that everyone will praise your heavenly Father."[65]

When I think of those words, I think of Preston Boutwell. His deeds shine brightly.

May God be praised.

---

[65] Mt. 5:14 NIV; Mt. 5:16 NLT, respectively

Part III

Most Important

- 21 -

THE LAMB

NOTHING IS MORE IMPORTANT THAN THIS

"For God so loved the world, that He gave His only begotten Son, that whoever believes in Him shall not perish, but have eternal life."

JOHN 3:16[66]

[66] NASB

Nothing Is More Important Than This

Six-year-old Sammy knew he was born for basketball. After school his ball was always with him—Sammy brought it to meals, bobbed it in his bath, and slept with it by his pillow. He'd even taught his parrot to speak his favorite word: Basketball!

With the tenacity of a mailman, Sam played in rain, snow, sleet, and gloom of night. After school, nothing came between him and his ball. Except that one day.

Thunder roared overhead, then lightning crackled and split the dark sky.

"Inside, Sammy!" his mom called.

The boy wandered from the living room to the dining room, ball on his hip. He sat at the kitchen window, rolling the ball on his knee. He stared at the sky, lightning still slicing the dark clouds. Before long, he began bouncing his ball.

"Sammy!" his mom called from somewhere in the house. "Dad told you no ball inside!"

The boy eyed the enclosed breezeway—he couldn't be heard out there.

"Okay!" he shouted.

And off he went, practicing his dribble, driving the ball between his legs, slamming it from hand to hand. It wasn't hurting anything. Until it did. The ball got away, hit the wall, and a picture came crashing down.

His dad eyed him that evening, and Sam saw the disappointment.

The next day little Sammy knew what he had to do.

"Can you fix it," he said in earnest, handing the frame across the counter at the hardware store. He hugged his piggybank under one arm.

The old clerk nodded, and Sam shoved all his treasure across the counter.

That night, Sam met his dad at the door with picture in hand. "I'm sorry."

His dad eyed him gently, scooping him into a hug. Sam started crying.

His dad leaned back. "Why so sad, son?"

Sam shook his head, choking on his tears. It was happiness—he and his dad were one again.

Maybe you remember disappointing a parent or grandparent. I remember those times vividly, the shame I felt. I couldn't wait to make it right.

Sammy eyed his dad who sat on his bed that night. "It's time you learned, Sam."

The boy climbed from under the covers and onto his dad's lap. "I paid for it."

"That's not how it works with God."

Sam slid his hand into his dad's. "How does it work?"

"Do you remember learning in Sunday school how God's people were in slavery in Egypt? How God parted the sea so they could flee?"

Sam nodded.

"But then they did terrible things. So God wrote a rulebook. It says what to do when the rules are broken. Disobeying Mom and me is in that rulebook."

The boy tightened his hand in his dad's.

"Sam, the only way a wrong can be wiped away between you and God is with a blood sacrifice."

Sammy straightened.

"God said to take an animal and kill it—a lamb, maybe a bird."

"It died?"

"It had to die. That was the price. Blood had to be shed. God's people needed to see how serious this was—they caused the animal to lose its life."

Sammy glanced toward his bird, big tears filling his eyes.

"God doesn't want Tweety's blood," his dad said. "Not anymore."

His dad lifted him and they knelt by the bed, but Sam didn't understand the words his father prayed.

Years passed and his dad often knelt with him at night, praying the same words. Sammy listened closely, but they never made sense to him.

"We ask forgiveness," his dad would say, "claiming Your sacrifice. Cover my son's wrongs that he might be restored to You."

One night, when Sam was twelve, he suddenly interrupted. "You're claiming the blood of Jesus. You're asking for Jesus' blood to cover my sins so I can be one again with God. Jesus was the sacrifice. Like the animal that was killed!"

"He's the Lamb of God, Sammy."

The boy understood it all now.

His dad went on. "Atonement is a great big word that just means 'At-One-ment.' You can break it apart and understand it easily, Sam. Jesus' crucifixion makes us at one with God if we believe."

Sammy's story is all important. His dad loves him—nothing the boy can do will ever change that. Nevertheless, when Sam disobeys his father, it separates them.

God loves us the same way, without condition. But disobedience separates us from our Father as surely as it separates Sam from his.

Ask for forgiveness, but that alone won't restore you to God—it's the blood of Christ that removes the wrong.

The Bible says: "If we confess our sins, he is faithful and just to forgive us our sins and to cleanse us . . . the blood of Jesus . . . cleanses us from all sin."[67]

That is the power of the crucifixion—Jesus' blood is the At-One-ment, restoring us to God.

Nothing in life is more important than this.

[67] I John 1:9,7 (ESV)

- 22 -

The Centurion

The Soldier's Famous Words of Faith

"Share in suffering as a good soldier of Christ Jesus."

2TIM. 2:3[68]

[68] ESV

The Soldier's Famous Words of Faith

He was not a young soldier. Not a private, first class. He'd risen through the ranks, the equivalent of a captain or major today. Scripture identifies him only as "the centurion," obviously a strong, brave man, and apparently in charge of Christ's crucifixion. He was both a disciplined soldier and one capable of great cruelty. The Roman army demanded such abilities.

When he awoke early that Friday morning, the centurion could not have known what the day would bring. Romans were heathens, worshipping gods and goddesses, but this soldier would soon speak one of the most famous statements of faith ever recorded in history.

Remember, Jesus is tried in the early morning hours by the Jews, then taken to Pilate who sends Him to Herod. Jesus is sent back to Pilate, condemned, and turned over to soldiers for execution.

The soldiers gather the whole Roman cohort, a battalion of men—perhaps 400. Two gospels describe almost word for word what happens next. It's remarkable. Apparently, those writers had a source among the soldiers—maybe the man who came to Christ that day.

Jesus is dressed in a fine robe. The soldiers twist together a crown of thorns, placing it on His head. They take a reed, putting it in His right hand. The soldiers kneel and bow before Him, shouting, "Hail King of the Jews!" They spit on Him, beating His head and face with that reed.[69]

Jesus is also scourged. He's beaten. The Roman whip had pieces of metal knotted into it, so as to tear open a man's flesh.

Jesus is taken to Golgotha where soldiers nail Him to the cross. The religious leaders had won, yet they come to the execution, jeering at our Lord, unable to let it go. Those passing also hurl abuse at Jesus. Even the soldiers make fun of our Lord: "If you are the King of the Jews, save yourself!"

Jesus responds, "Father, forgive them..."

When our Lord speaks these words, was it just for the Jews? Or did Jesus look also at the Roman soldiers—at the centurion? Did Jesus move this hardened soldier?

Scripture states the centurion came and stood at the foot of the cross, right in front of our Lord. A soldier of rank, there's little doubt he'd driven his sword through many men—from the coward fleeing battle to the opponent within arm's reach, taking a final breath to curse the centurion to his face. This commander wasn't prepared for a completely different Man. For Jesus.

Our Lord shouts, "It is finished. Father into Your Hands I commit My Spirit." [70]

And Jesus breathes His last.

---

[69] Mt. 27:27-30, Mark 15:16-19

[70] John 19:30, Luke 23:46 (NASB)

Scripture says the centurion begins praising God.[71]

And at this moment he speaks his famous statement of faith. I'll let the Bible tell you:

"When the centurion, who was standing right in front of [Jesus], saw the way He breathed His last, he said, 'Truly this man was the Son of God!'"[72]

The centurion saw Jesus seek forgiveness for those who'd bitterly abused Him. It changed the man.

The ability to truly forgive is a great divider of men and women. Ministers will tell you it's a troubling problem within their congregations.

The matter can cut even deeper.

I am reminded of a small church I attended years ago. Our new minister—the most gifted speaker I'd ever heard—seemed destined to become a world-renowned evangelist. When he preached, you could hear a pin drop.

Yet something seemed amiss. He was nearly forty and hadn't been assigned a larger church.

Soon enough, those beautifully-delivered sermons became a problem. Church attendance dwindled.

One Sunday, a deacon approached me, frowning. "The things he says."

"Have you talked to him?" I asked.

He nodded and scowled, even more upset.

"What happens now?" I asked.

"We're stuck with him."

So what was the minister's problem? Here's an example. During Bible study the minister mentioned a man who'd wronged him.

---

[71] Luke 23:47 (NASB)

[72] Mark 15:39 (NASB)

"That jerk!" he said.

See what I mean—the minister hadn't learned to forgive.

As I said, he's not alone. We live in a world that teaches fairness, and forgiveness is the epitome of unfairness—the wrongdoer doesn't deserve to be forgiven.

Every day, remember the crushing death of our Lord. Know that you are His witness to the world. Remember also the centurion standing before the cross, how forgiveness changed his life.

The greater the ordeal, the greater the impact of forgiveness on another.

Hold dear this Bible verse. Memorize it and keep it close: "Share in suffering as a good soldier of Christ Jesus."[73]

Do as Jesus did. Forgive.

---

[73] 2Tim. 2:3 (ESV)

- 23 -

THE MESSIAH

THE FINAL WORDS OF CHRIST

"My God, my God, why have You forsaken me?"

PSALM 22:1[74]

[74] NASB

The Final Words of Christ

The dying thoughts of any man are significant but much more so when they belong to Christ.

Jesus made seven statements on the cross, and one has become the subject of many Easter sermons: "My God, my God, why have you forsaken me?"

Preachers often explain by saying Jesus took upon Himself all the sins of the world, and God had to turn away. Ask these same ministers if God is almighty and they will say, "Absolutely!"

Omnipotence means God doesn't have to do anything. No amount of sin would be too much for Him. So why say it? Why have many Christians come to accept this limitation on God?

Because we hold Scripture dear, and Jesus said these words—so they must be understood.

I have heard others explain by saying, "Jesus just wanted it over."

Indeed, but that's not the same as claiming Jesus thought God had forsaken Him.

My Lutheran friend explained how her church teaches it. "God definitely didn't leave Jesus," she said. "But our Lord was overwhelmed and *thought* God had left Him."

Completely at odds with the facts.

Was Jesus overwhelmed when stakes were driven into his hands and feet? If our Lord had thought God had deserted Him, this would have been the time.

Instead, look at what Jesus does.

He thinks of his mother's future. Jesus says to her, "...behold, your son!," indicating his beloved disciple. And then Jesus says to the disciple, "Behold, your mother!" [75]

Our Lord comforts the thief saying, "...today, you will be with Me in Paradise."[76]

Jesus even thinks of those jeering at Him. "Father," He says, "forgive them, for they know not what they do."[77]

And it is Jesus who gives up His own spirit. "Father, into your hands I commit my spirit!"[78] Then Jesus breathes His last.

Our Lord is in control every moment He hangs on the cross.

So if God did not abandon Christ, and if Jesus never felt abandoned, why did our Lord say, "My God, my God, why have you forsaken me?"[79]

The Jews who stood at the foot of the cross would have known exactly.

Their hope for the Messiah was much greater than ours, as was their understanding of the Old Testament. Moreover, in Jesus' day the Psalms were not neatly numbered because of the competing influence of the

---

[75] John 19: 26, 27 (ESV)

[76] Luke 23:43 (ESV)

[77] Luke 23:34 (ESV)

[78] Luke 23:46 (ESV)

[79] Mark 15:34 (ESV)

Greek version of the Bible. So, when a teacher referred to a Psalm, he could not say "Psalm 23." Instead, he would speak the first line.

The first line of Psalm 22 reads: "My God, my God, why have you forsaken me?" Saying those words was the equivalent of saying "Psalm 22." Jesus had merely identified a Psalm to his listeners. Not anything more. Nothing ominous!

The Bible confirms this—the word Jesus uses for God proves He was quoting Scripture. Without delving into Greek, Hebrew, and Aramaic, suffice it to say Jesus spoke to God saying, *Father***.** It was close and personal.

If Jesus had been addressing God in this statement about being forsaken, why did Jesus abruptly switch to a formal, Old Testament word for God? And that word happens to be the exact same word used in Psalm 22.

Jesus wasn't speaking to God about being forsaken—He was quoting Psalm 22.

The beloved disciple also confirms this. Remember that John is an eyewitness to the crucifixion, yet John chooses to leave the forsaken words out of his Gospel.

Why would John do that?

John wrote his text last and perhaps was aware that non-Jews were having trouble understanding these last words of Jesus, just as we stumble with them today. Instead of repeating Jesus' statement, John quotes Psalm 22, showing how it relates to Jesus:

So the [guards] said to one another, "Let us not tear [the tunic], but cast lots for it to decide whose it shall be"; this was to fulfill the Scripture "They divided My outer garments among them, and for My clothing they cast lots."[80]

---

[80] John 19:24 (NASB) quoting Psalm 22:18

In other words, John points the reader to Psalm 22 just as Jesus had done!

But why was Psalm 22 so important to our Lord, considering everything He might have chosen from Scripture?

Because it said everything.

For a thousand years, God's people had sung Psalm 22. They knew those words by heart. They knew Psalm 22 promised the Messiah. Now, the Jews at the crucifixion could see the Psalm happening before them.

The Roman soldiers had nailed Jesus' hands and feet to the cross.

The Psalm says: "...they have pierced my hands and feet." Psalm 22:16 (ESV)

Jesus' bones would have been out of joint from hanging from nails.

The Psalm says: "I can count all my bones—" Psalm 22:17 (ESV)

And we've already seen how the Psalm says that the Romans would gamble for Jesus' clothes.

But Psalm 22 does much more than promise the Messiah. It claims the Lord will be told to coming generations, to a people yet unborn—that all the ends of the earth would turn to the Lord. The Psalm ends triumphantly, and the Jews would have known that.

Today, there are more Christians in the world than adherents to any other faith.

When Jesus said "Psalm 22," He thereby said, "I am the promised Messiah and this is God's victory!"

Jesus could not have said more, nor said it better.

- 24 -

SIMON PETER

BREAKFAST ON THE BEACH WITH THE RISEN LORD

"If we confess our sins, He is faithful and just and will forgive us…"

I JOHN 1:9[81]

[81] NIV

Breakfast on the Beach with the Risen Lord

At six years old, Billy could count change. He could also be a handful.

"Ninety cents!" He giggled, counting the dimes as his mother drove away from the little country store. He'd brought a dollar for candy and should have had only pennies left. "Miss Ruby is blind as a bat!"

His mother abruptly made a U-turn, parked, and marched him inside.

"But I didn't do anything!" he said.

She eyed him harshly. "Tell Miss Ruby you took her money."

The old woman toddled slowly from the rear of the store. "What's this?"

At 96, she had worked there since before the Depression.

"I took it." Billy opened his hand with the change. "You gave me dimes instead of pennies."

The woman examined the money closely, adjusting her glasses.

"Billy," his mom said. "Apologize for the rest."

He swallowed hard as they waited, tears rising in his eyes. "I said...something..."

His mother nudged him.

"Blind as a bat," he blurted out, then buried his head in the old woman's skirts, sobbing. "I'm sorry. I take it back!"

She gently lifted his face, wiping the tears with her apron. "Reckon I've said worse. You're sorry, so that's that."

Decades later, Billy said, "That experience broke me open—it changed my life."

Not long after Jesus' resurrection, such shame would break open another heart.

It's daybreak and our risen Lord stands alone on the beach of a large lake, waiting. He's built a charcoal fire, grilling bread and fish. There's important business to finish.

A boat appears offshore. Jesus knows the seven fishermen onboard, knows they've been up all night without a catch. He calls out, telling them to move the net, and it quickly fills with fish.

"Come and have breakfast," Jesus says to them.

Our Lord takes bread and fish from the fire and feeds them. After breakfast, he eyes Peter.

"Do you love Me...?" Jesus asks.

"Yes, Lord; You know that I love You." Peter answers.

Jesus asks again, and Peter must have looked at Jesus deeply. "Yes, Lord," Peter says, again.

But it's the third time that hurts—Jesus has just placed Simon Peter's shame into that disciple's hands. Peter had denied Jesus three times in the courtyard and has never confessed his regret.

Jesus had to break Peter, one way or another.

"Do you love me?" Jesus asks three times.

Peter gets the message. Oh, yes. Scripture tells us plainly: "Peter was grieved because [Jesus] said to him the third time, 'Do you love me?'"[82]

Many think Peter denied Jesus because of fear. No. Jesus knew what it was.

Remember, Peter drew his sword and sliced off the ear of Malchus, the high priest's man leading those with weapons who'd come for Jesus. Peter would have fought and died for our Lord.

That wasn't what Jesus wanted.

Our Lord surrendered, telling his captors to let the disciples go.

Peter finds a way into the courtyard where Jesus has been taken, needing to stay close. He then denies Jesus to avoid detection. Only when the cock crows does Peter realize his mistake—Jesus turns and looks at him. Right then, Peter still could have said, "I'm with Him."

Instead, Simon Peter went out and wept.

Peter knew no fear. He would have died for Jesus, but he couldn't surrender. Peter had too much pride—surrender was weakness.

Now, here on this beach, Jesus wants to know, "Do you love me, Peter?" Can you follow me? Will you surrender yourself this time?

Recently, a woman came and apologized to me. She knew I'd overheard something she'd said. I could see how much it hurt her.

When you regret your misdeeds, when you come forward and say, "I'm sorry," it will break you open.

Billy said, "I never wanted to go through it again."

---

[82] John 21:17 (NASB)

Because the apology changes us, God says confess your sins.[83]

Confession has broken me many times. It should hurt. If you can easily tell God your misdeeds, I ask whether you truly love Jesus. You should see your wrongs and say, "Jesus died for this?"

Apologize to those you hurt—it will help them, it will help you more.

And always, say you're sorry to God.

[83] 1 John 1:9

READ FREE

Read a new truth each week free and help your community at the same time!

Ask your newspaper publisher and editor to print a great truth in your local paper. Believe me, selling newspapers can be tough work and knowing what you like is usually a top priority for publishers and editors. Surprisingly, many think no one wants to read about Jesus.

One such editor often asks me to pray for his crime-ridden community. He's a devout Christian, but he refuses to publish a weekly column about Jesus. That seems amazing to me.

Not so amazing is another big-time editor who is a Buddhist. He won't publish pieces about Christ because they seem to offend him. He doesn't realize that his readers are Christian—that he is publishing to gain readership, not to please his preference.

I tell them both: It's all about Jesus!

Join my voice.

Call or send your newspaper editor and publisher an e-mail now. Tell each that a Christian faith column is what you want to read and what your community needs.

Every week we will send articles to your newspaper at no charge—all your publisher/editor has to do is send a request to:

ReachingToGod.com

Talk to your editor today!

DEEP DISCOUNTS FOR GROUPS

Contact us if you would like a wholesale price for books for your church. Pass along the savings to your members or use the book as a fundraiser for your Sunday School project, mission project, or youth group.

Civic and other organizations should also contact us for wholesale pricing for books for their fundraising projects.

Visit us online:

ReachingToGod.com

A FINAL THOUGHT

Share with others.

If this book has helped you, write about it on Amazon. Your words might encourage another person. It's easy, 3 little steps:

1. Go to Amazon.com
2. Type in the search window: Reaching to God: Great Truths from the Bible
3. Scroll down and click *Write a Review*.

It's easy!

LOOK FOR OTHER TITLES

by

R.A. Matthews

Reaching To God:
Great Truths from the Bible
Volume 2

Emerald Coast:
To Kill an Actress

A Christian Thriller told in serial volumes

Coming in
2017 & 2018

Made in United States
Orlando, FL
24 February 2022